TWAYNE'S WORLD AUTHORS SERIES

A Survey of the World's Literature

Sylvia E. Bowman, Indiana University

GENERAL EDITOR

CHINA

William E. Schultz, University of Arizona

EDITOR

Yüan Chen

TWAS 442

Yüan Chen

Copy from the reproduction of an ancient painting,
copied by Chang Wen-i.

YÜAN CHEN

By ANGELA C. Y. JUNG PALANDRI
University of Oregon

TWAYNE PUBLISHERS
A DIVISION OF G. K. HALL & CO., BOSTON

Library of Congress Cataloging in Publication Data

Palandri, Angela C   Y   Jung, 1926–
    Yüan Chen.

    (Twayne's world authors series; TWAS 442: China)
    Bibliography: pp. 191–96
    Includes index.
    1. Yüan, Chen, 779–831. 2. Authors, Chinese—
Biography.
PL2677.Y8Z8   1977   895.1'1'3 [B]   77–3453
ISBN 0–8057–6279–5

Contents

About the Author

Angela C. Y. Jung Palandri is Professor of Chinese and chairperson of the Department of Chinese and Japanese, University of Oregon. A native of China, she received her B.A. from the Fu Jen University of Peking, and her Ph.D. from the University of Washington. She is the author of two volumes of translations of Chinese poetry: *Sun-and-Moon Collection* (Taipei: Mei-ya Publishers, 1968) and *Modern Verse from Taiwan* (Berkeley and Los Angeles: University of California Press, 1972.) She is a frequent contributor to various literary and scholarly journals, such as *Literature East & West, Comparative Literature, West Coast Review* (Canada), *Northwest Review, Contemporary Literature in Translation* (Canada), *Tamkang Review: A Journal of Comparative Literature* (Taiwan), *Italian Quarterly,* and *Il Veri* (Italy). She has written several articles on Yüan Chen, and some of her earlier translations of Yüan Chen's poems have been included in *Sunflower Splendor* (Doubleday, 1974). She lives with her husband and two children in Eugene, Oregon.

Preface

The T'ang dynasty (618–906) has been generally recognized as the "Golden Age" of Chinese poetry. For, like the prose of the Han dynasty (B.C. 206–221 A.D.), the calligraphy of the Chin dynasty (265–419), the painting of the Sung dynasty (907–1234), and the porcelain of the Ming dynasty (1368–1644), T'ang poetry represents the culmination of China's cultural attainment in a special art form with universal appeal transcending temporal, spatial, and racial limits. It is outstanding both in quantity and quality. The *Ch'üan T'ang Shih* (a complete anthology of T'ang poetry) compiled by Ts'ao Yin (1658–1712) during the Ch'ing dynasty, contains approximately 48,900 poems by some 2200 T'ang poets. Even if not all of these poems are poetry *par excellence,* there are sufficient poems of high quality to suit the taste and fancy of all poetry lovers. Consequently, T'ang poetry has received greater attention at home and abroad than Chinese poetry of any other era.

In *From the Chinese* (Oxford, 1945), R. C. Trevelyan said, "Among the poets of the T'ang dynasty, the most important are Li Po (ca. 701–762), Tu Fu (712–770), and Po Chü-i (772–846)."* Indeed this is the customary view, since these three are the most frequently anthologized poets both in Chinese and in translation. Of particular interest is the increasing popularity of Po Chü-i in the English speaking world, as evidenced by, and perhaps because of, Arthur Waley's translations and his sympathetic biographical account in *The Life and Times of Po Chü-i* (London, 1949). This was followed by Eugene Feifel's book, *Po Chü-i As A Censor* (New York, 1954), and, more recently, by Howard S. Levy's two volume *Translations from Po Chü-i's Collected Works* (New York, 1971). By contrast, Yüan Chen (779–831), who in his lifetime shared the literary limelight with Po Chü-i, has been overshadowed by his friend and rival

---

*R.C. Trevelyan, *From the Chinese* (Oxford, 1945), p. vii.

to the extent that Po Chü-i is accorded full credit for their col-
laborative literary efforts, in spite of the fact that Yüan Chen
was in most cases the initiator of their joint literary undertakings.

Apparently time and history have conspired to bring about
Yüan Chen's literary eclipse. Indeed, within a hundred years
after his death, a large portion of his works was lost. Practically
nothing he wrote before 800 and after 825 is preserved for
posterity. The main corpus of his extant writings, the *Yüan-shih
Ch'ang-ch'ing chi* (Yüan's Collected Works), handed down from
a Northern Sung manuscript copied by Liu Lin (dated 1124 in
the preface), consists of only sixty *chüan* of the original collection of one hundred *chüan* compiled by the poet himself in
823. And of the hundred and more "romantic poems" (*yen-shih*)
mentioned by Yüan Chen in 813, only fifty-seven are extant,
thanks to Wei Ku's (fl. 934–964) anthology, *Ts'ai-tiao chi* or
Voices of Geniuses. In all, less than six hundred of Yüan Chen's
poems have been handed down to us, whereas the poems he
exchanged with Po Chü-i alone exceeded that number.

It is difficult for us at this distance in time to determine
whether this loss was the cause or the consequence of the neglect
the poet suffered. From his literary remains it is easy to see
that he deserves greater critical attention. At present only a
fraction of Yüan Chen's poems has been translated into English.
He is also omitted from many Chinese poetry anthologies. Why
is he ignored? What is his intrinsic literary merit? Does his
personality or his politics have any bearing on the traditional
attitude or bias toward him? The present volume grew out
of my curiosity. The principal aim of this study is to examine
Yüan Chen's life and works with an open mind. Since little
objective and accurate biographical data are available, it is
necessary to let Yüan Chen speak for himself through his own
writings. For this reason I have allowed considerable space for
his poetry, which represents his own testimonial to his social
identity and personal emotions. I also wish to add that in the
interest of continuity, I have confined my discussion of historical
references and literary allusions to the Notes and References
section.

I am indebted to Professor Hideki Hanabusa of Kyoto for
sending me three volumes of his Yüan Chen studies (see

Preface

Bibliography) which were otherwise inaccessible to me. I also owe a debt to David Kellog for his suggestion that I write to Hanabusa after all interlibrary loan channels had been explored. I am grateful to James Tang, librarian, and his staff at the East Asiatic Library, University of California, Berkeley, and to Jane Hsu of the University of Oregon Library, for their assistance during the early stages of my research; to Professors Wu-chi Liu of Indiana University, Vincent Shih of the University of Washington, and Chia-ying Yeh Chao of the University of British Columbia, for verification of certain classical allusions in Yüan Chen's poems; to Keith Ewing, Michael B. Fish, and most of all, my husband, Guido Palandri, for reading part of my first draft. I wish to thank Professor William Schultz of the University of Arizona, editor of the Chinese section of the Twayne World Authors Series, for his patient editing and confidence in seeing the task through. A summer faculty research grant from the Office of Scholarly and Scientific Research of the Graduate School of the University of Oregon made it possible for me to devote an entire summer to the research. For permission to use three of my own translations and Professor Liu's "Song of the Weaving Woman," which appeared in *Sunflower Splendor*, New York: Doubleday. Copyright 1975, by Wu-chi Liu and Irving Lo, I am indebted to both the editors and the publisher. I alone am responsible for all inaccuracies and errors in this book.

Chronology

799   Born in Ch'ang-an.

786   His father Yüan K'uan died; his mother, née Cheng, began to supervise his studies.

787–   Learned to compose poetry; the family moved to Feng-
788   hsiang, Shensi.

793   Passed the first civil service examination in the *ming-ching* category ("explication of the classics").

794   Returned to Ch'ang-an, possibly from Feng-hsiang.

802   Married Wei Hui-ts'ung; won first place in the "placing examination" (*pa-ts'ui*); appointed collator of texts in the imperial library.

806   Passed the "palace examination" (*chih-k'e tui-ts'e*); promoted to censor of the left (*tso shih-yi*) in the chancellery; demoted and ordered to Ho-nan as a magistrate on the tenth of the ninth month, but his mother died on the sixteenth of the same month and Yüan Chen retired from office to observe the prescribed mourning period.

809   Appointed inspecting censor (*chien-ch'a yü-shih*) on special mission to the circuit of Tung Ch'uan (in Szechwan); transferred in the eighth month to Lo-yang to head the eastern branch office of the censorate; his wife died while he was away from home.

810   Removed from office and demoted to marshal at Chiang-ling in the third month.

812   Edited his own poems (over eight hundred titles) and arranged them into twenty *chüan* or fascicles.

815   Transferred to T'ung-chou (in Szechwan); sick with malaria for months.

817   Wrote *yüeh-fu* songs with ancient titles; possibly composed the *Lien-ch'ang kung tz'u* in the same year.

819   Transferred to Kuo-chou as senior secretary (*ch'ang-shih*); recalled to Ch'ang-an and given the title assis-

tant secretary of the imperial banquet board (*shan-pu yüan-wai-lang*).

820   Received the title of assistant secretary of the board of imperial worship (*Tz'u-pu lang-chung*).

821   Promoted on the sixteenth of the second month to *chih chih-kao*, heading the academy in charge of drafting imperial proclamations and rescripts; became assistant minister of the Ministry of Labor on the nineteenth of the tenth month.

822   Promoted to chief minister on the nineteenth of the second month; removed from the post on the fifth of the sixth month and sent to T'ung-chou (in modern Shensi) as commissioner (*kuan-ch'a shih*).

823   Appointed inspector general of the Che-tung district circuit, centering around Yüeh-chou; selected and edited his own works into one hundred *chüan*, entitled *Yüan-shih ch'ang-ch'ing chi*.

824–   Completed editing Po Chü-i's collected works, which
825   he named *Po-shih ch'ang-ch'ing chi;* its introduction is dated the tenth of the twelfth month.

827   Received the title of assistant or auxiliary vice-minister of the Ministry of Rites on the eighteenth of the ninth month.

829   Received the honorary title minister of state (*shang-shu tso-ch'eng*).

830   Received the title of minister of the board of revenue (*hu-pu shang-shu*) in the first month; assigned to duty as governor of Wu-ch'ang, concurrently retaining the former duty of imperial commissioner of Yüeh-chou.

831   Died on the twenty-second of the seventh month in Wu-chang; his body sent back to Hsien-yang for burial; received the posthumous title minister of state (*shang-shu yu-p'u-she*).

CHAPTER 1

Social and Political Background

TO understand Yüan Chen the poet as well as the man, it is necessary that we have some background knowledge of the time in which he lived; for every person is a product of his time, whether he happens to go along with or against the prevailing tide, whether he lags behind or advances ahead of the on-rushing current.

The T'ang dynasty (618–906), of which the Chinese speak with pride even to this day, is one of the most glorious periods in the history of China. During the first half of the eighth century, prior to the An Lu-shan—Shih Szu-ming Rebellion (755–763),[1] which shook the very foundations of the T'ang empire, China was the superpower of Asia, enjoying peace and prosperity and international prestige, in a way paralleling the position of the United States in the twentieth century. The imperial capital, Ch'ang-an (modern Sian in Shensi), was also known as the Western Capital (as opposed to the Eastern Capital, Lo-yang in Honan, which had been the capital of the Toba-Wei dynasty during the Age of Disunity prior to the unification of the Sui Dynasty in 581). It was the center of high fashion and civilization of the eastern hemisphere, teeming with tourists, merchants, monks, missionaries, and emissaries from many nations. Indigenous talents such as poets, musicians, and learned scholars also gathered in this great metropolis, because it was also a seat of higher culture and education and a gateway to officialdom.

During the first month of each year, two civil examinations were administered: the classical examination (*ming-ching*, literally "explication of the classics"), and the literary examination upon the successful passing of which the candidate would become an "advanced scholar" (*chin-shih*). In addition, special examinations were given by the board of civil affairs, and even

13

more prestigious examinations were administered in the palace, supposedly by the emperor himself.[2] The cultural development of T'ang times reached its apogee during the Hsüan-tsung emperor's reign (r. 713–756), comparable in some ways to the Periclean age (ca. 495–429 B.C) of ancient Greece for its intellectual activities and brilliant achievements. Small wonder that almost every scholar dreamed of going to the capital to participate in the civil service examinations, for passing the examinations had become practically the only road to public distinction, wealth, and officialdom, especially for those who bore no hereditary titles. Every scholar with worldly ambition would have liked to become an official, whether his motive was to serve the people and the state or to gain personal fame and fortune. Moreover, every official in the empire wished to be in or near Ch'ang-an. Aside from its being the site of the imperial court with all its attendant glamour and magnificence, Ch'ang-an was the hub of all cultural and political activities, where all the important decisions affecting the lives of the populace were made. Thus, transfer from a government position in the capital to one in the provinces was generally regarded as banishment, and banishment from Ch'ang-an was regarded as punishment. The more serious the crime the further removed from the capital was the banished official. Frequently some of those who were banished to the southern malaria-ridden districts died at their posts.

The An-Shih Rebellion marks a key turning point in T'ang history. It broke out during the last year of the Hsüan-tsung emperor's reign. Both the Eastern and Western capitals were sacked by the rebels. Hsüan-tsung fled from Ch'ang-an to Szechwan with his court. But when they reached the Ma-wei post station, not far from the capital, the imperial guards mutinied and demanded that the emperor surrender his favorite concubine, Yang Kuei-fei (718–756), who, along with her cousin the Chief Minister Yang Kuo-chung (d. 756), was blamed for the national disaster. There were many causes, of course, for this rebellion, but the most tangible and immediate, though not logical, target seems to have been Yang Kuei-fei herself. It was alleged that she had so infatuated the aging emperor that he neglected affairs of state and left the administration in the hands of incompetent rascals like Yang Kuo-chung. Furthermore, it was through her patronage that the semibarbarian rebel, An Lu-shan (d. 757), had been vested with great military powers as a commander-in-chief of Hopei, where he rose in rebellion. The helpless emperor could not but yield to the brutal demand, and allowed Yang Kuei-fei to be strangled. Only then was the emperor escorted to safety in Szechwan, where he was forced to abdicate in favor of his son Su-tsung. The rebellion was finally put down, but not without enlisting military aid from the Uigur and Turkish tribes, thus "opening the doors to the wolves" and new foreign invasions.

Eight years of civil war caused by the An-Shih Rebellion not only drastically reduced the size of the Chinese empire, but the population as well. Moreover, the national treasury was depleted; since much of the nation lay in waste, revenue resources were also seriously drained. The devastation was such that later attempts to restore the nation politically and economically were only nominally successful, and the dynasty continued to decline until it finally disintegrated in 906.

The political instability that marked the last century and a half of T'ang rule was symbolized by the quick succession with which one emperor succeeded another during Yüan Chen's lifetime. In 779, the year of Yüan Chen's birth, the Tai-tsung emperor died. Te-tsung (r. 780–805), who succeeded him, had an exceptionally long reign. However, these years were beset with continuing insurrections by the provincial military governors. Ch'ang-an was sacked once more in 783 by mutinous troops. And the Tibetans, who also took advantage of China's internal troubles and military weakness, revolted and marched to the capital. A hard line policy toward the provinces, and the demand for more tribute and exorbitant taxation, only brought more hardship upon the common people, who, in turn, rose in revolt. The bureaucrats in the court were divided in their views regarding the policies of the central government toward the outlying districts. During the brief reign of the Shun-tsung emperor in 805, the government fell into the hands of Wang Shu-wen (d. 812) and Wang Pi (d. 805), both men of special talents, but also men of plebeian origin who could not command the support of the conservative ruling party. Factions at court, divided politically and by social origin, became so strong that the entire administration was threatened. The Shun-tsung emperor was forced to abdicate after eight months of political turmoil.[3]

The *yüan-ho* era was inaugurated in 806 under the Hsien-tsung emperor (r. 806–820), who came to the throne with eunuch and military backing. The first political act of Hsien-tsung was an attempt to sweep the court clear of political factions. He was unable, however, to rid the court of those eunuchs who were responsible for his elevation to the throne. Meanwhile, under his own administration, new cliques formed around the aristocratic scholar-officials of the traditional hereditary ruling class on the one side, and newcomers or *parvenus* on the other. The latter, as a rule, were young intellectuals, whose backgrounds and sympathies identified them with the common people, whose causes they tended to espouse. It is to this new faction that Yüan Chen seems to have belonged, although by lineage he was a descendant of the imperial house of the Toba-Wei (386–532) that ruled North China during the Southern and Northern dynasties.[4]

The so-called "new faction" to which Yüan Chen belonged, or was at least related by association, was led by Niu Seng-ju (779–848) and Li Tsung–min (d. 806), who represented the young intellectuals then rising to power through the examination system.[5] They were more conscious of the sufferings of the people caused by official injustice and corruption, and they believed that social and political rather than military solutions were needed to remedy the nation's ills. Opposed to the government's frequent military campaigns, they perceived that military spending and conscription, with considerable disruption in the daily lives of the people, could only weaken the national economy and further endanger the security of the state. There would have been no revolts, they argued, had there been a benevolent government free from corruption, with only the welfare of its people in mind, as long ago prescribed by Confucius.

The opposing faction was led by Li Te-yü (787–850), son of the Chief Minister Li Chi-fu (758–812), who represented conservative elements with long ties of association to the imperial house and hereditary titles dating back to the founding of the dynasty. This group, predominantly from the Shantung nobility, believed in hard line policies and the maintenance of the status quo, and advocated suppression of dissident factions both at home and abroad by military means, if necessary.[6]

The struggle for political power between these two factions, intensified by personal feuds among the party leaders, continued for almost fifty years, and weakened the bureaucratic structure upon which the empire rested and strengthened further the power of the eunuchs who had entrenched themselves in the central administration and the armies. Hsien-tsung, caught up in the power struggles within his administration, acted in the only way open to him: he employed both the old and new factions by turns, i.e., he put one party in power until its failures led to its removal, in which case the opposing party was ordered to take over. To stabilize its own position, each party tried to enlist the support of influential eunuchs. It was in this volatile political environment that Yüan Chen began his own official career. It is small wonder, then, that his political career fluctuated between high office and demotion and banishment.

Of the six emperors who ruled during Yüan Chen's lifetime,[7] the Mu-tsung emperor (r. 821–824), who succeeded Hsien-tsung, showered him with special favors and raised him to the position of chief minister. But party factionalism, eunuch intrigue, and power politics were endemic, and even the emperor could not protect him from obloquy. Despite his brilliance as an administrator with high ideals, Yüan Chen was regarded, after all, as an "upstart," a *parvenu*. His pacifist policies antagonized the "palace guard," who believed that the authority of the central government must be restored by force. Moreover, in his zeal to clean up the government, he made war against corruption and extortion wherever he found them. As a consequence of his exposure of illegal dealings and corruption in high places, he aroused the wrath of powerful political leaders and eunuch factions.[8] Had Yüan Chen remained in the position of chief minister longer, it is possible he might have been able to accomplish some of the things he originally set out to do. But his term in office lasted only a few months.

Mu-tsung's reign was a brief one. He died at the age of twenty-nine, a victim of the so-called elixirs of immortality. The

two emperors that followed (Ching-tsung, r. 824–827; and
Wen-tsung, r. 827–840) were unable to stem the tide, and the
end came in 906, caused in part by the devastating Huang Ch'ao
Rebellion (881–883).[9]

Despite a deteriorating situation in national politics and the
administration following the An Lu-shan Rebellion, progress continued to be made in certain sectors. Trade with the West continued to flourish. China was at this time receptive to foreign
influences, especially in music and other forms of popular entertainment. There was also greater religious tolerance than was
generally characteristic of earlier or later times. Not only were
foreigners allowed to live in China and to build their churches
and temples, but they were free to propagate their faith among
the Chinese people without undue interference. Among
those members of the scholar class who publicly espoused Confucianism, there also seemed to be less rigidity in philosophical
outlook. Many T'ang poets, for instance, were eclectic-minded.
They professed to be Confucians when in public office; in
private life, however, they adhered to the Taoist philosophy
of naturalism in their acceptance of life and its natural processes,
and they sought in Buddhism the existential quality of Ch'anism
(Zen) and detachment from worldly concerns. At first glance,
there would seem to be irreconcilable differences between these
religio-philosophical concepts. But when taken in proper perspective, and kept in proper balance, all could serve a useful purpose in life. However, when those engaged in official capacities
came under the influence of the superstitious practices of popular
Buddhism and Taoism to the point of neglecting their social
responsibilities, then there was cause for concern.

Since Confucianism was the backbone of the bureaucratic
system of the T'ang empire, which was patterned after the
structure of the Han dynasty, the T'ang officials attempted to
reinforce Confucian ideology to offset the inordinate influences
of Taoism and Buddhism. Many of the emperors came under
the influence of Taoism and Buddhism, and the consequences
were both neglect of state affairs and occasionally unintentional
self-destruction (by taking so-called "pills of immortality").
Orthodox Confucian doctrine insisted that man was by nature
morally good and therefore amenable to education; that the

raison d'être of government was to serve the people; that the ruler and those who governed were to be virtuous and exemplary in their personal conduct; that while laws and punishments were necessary, they should be flexible and subordinate to the moral law; that all government policies and services should be based on the teachings expounded in the Confucian classics; that the state could prosper only if the people believed in the emperor and his possession of the mandate of heaven; that the ministers served the emperor loyally, but did not shirk from criticizing or remonstrating with the emperor whenever necessary, even at great personal risk.[10]

If the Confucian precepts were not fully realized and put into practice throughout the T'ang period, they were, at least in theory, guidelines for the government administration. For this reason, candidates for the civil service examinations were frequently tested on their knowledge and application of the Confucian classics. Moreover, in some instances, special examinations were administered in the palace for the purpose of seeking out men of talent and courage who could offer constructive criticism and fresh and innovative ideas in matters concerning the government. Even if the Confucian precepts existed only in theory, Yüan Chen seems to have taken his Confucian training more seriously than most, at least during his early years, which may, in part, account for his checkered career.

CHAPTER 2

Biographical Sketch

YÜAN Chen (courtesy name: Wei-chih) was a complex person with a complicated family background. He was born in 779, but no exact date of birth is recorded in the historical records. All historians consider him a native of Lo-yang, Honan, not because he was actually born there, but rather, according to Chinese tradition, because Lo-yang was the place where his ancestors chose to settle down. It is recorded in the T'ang histories that Yüan Chen was a tenth generation descendant of the royal family of the Toba-Wei dynasty which ruled northern China during the fifth and sixth centuries.[1] One of its rulers, Hsiao Wen-ti (r. 471–495), anxious to be assimilated into the mainstream of Chinese culture, had adopted "Yüan" (meaning "the beginning," or "primal") as the Chinese surname for his clan, and had moved the capital from P'ing-ch'eng (in Shansi) to Lo-yang. During the unification of China under the Sui dynasty (605–618), the offspring of the Toba house remained in Lo-yang. These people of alien extraction were not discriminated against by the Chinese during the T'ang dynasty as foreigners; they were referred to simply as "people of Lo-yang." Most probably, Yüan Chen was born in Ch'ang-an, where his father, Yüan K'uan (d. 786), held a minor post on the board of justice, and later became senior secretary in the household of Prince Shu.[2] Although his great-great-grandfather had been president of the Ministry of War during the Sui dynasty, no one in his family during T'ang times could claim any scholarly distinction prior to the rise of Yüan Chen.[3]

I The Early Years of a High Achiever

Poverty in ancient China was (and perhaps still is) considered a virtue rather than a vice according to the Confucian tradition.

It was therefore conventional for Chinese scholar-officials to make exaggerated claims to poverty, possibly as an indication that they lived above corruption, bribery, and extortion, which were the common means to wealth. However, when Yüan Chen spoke of his poverty-stricken childhood, it was most likely true. His father died in 786, when Yüan Chen was only seven years old (eight according to the Chinese way of counting age). The family was left destitute. Yüan Chen's mother, née Cheng, daughter of Cheng Chi (fl. 740–790), a minister in the imperial court,[4] had to take upon herself the double responsibility of rearing and educating her children, not, however, without support from her own father and brothers. In a letter to his nephews, Yüan Chen mentioned that all his father left the family was "pure poverty," and for a time they were dependent on his maternal uncle.[5] Between 789 and 793 Yüan Chen was in Feng-hsiang, Shensi, where his brother-in-law, Lu Han, was magistrate of Hsia-yang.[6]

Yüan Chen passed the civil examination under the category "clarification of the classics" in 793, when he was only fourteen years of age, the youngest age one was admitted to the examinations. The degree, not a prestigious one, qualified him to hold minor, temporary positions, which enabled him to provide for his family. This could have been the reason for his taking the classical examination instead of the literary examination which required more preparation and would have been intellectually more taxing for a youth of fourteen. Undoubtedly, Yüan Chen was precocious. In several accounts he tells us that under his mother's instruction he was able to write poems at the age of eight. His elders (the maternal grandfather and his cronies) were deeply impressed by his poetic talent. Soon he began to receive daily instructions on prosody from the famous poet Yang Chü-yüan (780–832).[7] By the time he was fourteen he had mastered all the rules of tonal euphony in versification.[8]

What else Yüan Chen did besides studying and writing poetry between the ages of fifteen and twenty-two is not mentioned in the official records. There does exist, however, a famous short story, "Meeting with the Immortal" (*Hui-chen chi*), which is also known as "The Story of Ying-ying" (*Ying-ying chuan*), traditionally believed to be autobiographical.[9] If this work can be so taken, we may surmise that he frequented Po-chou, the capital of the prefecture that lay between Feng-hsiang and Ch'ang-an. And during one of his excursions he retreated to a monastery for a period of study, there to prepare for the metropolitan examinations. There he became involved in a brief but passionate love affair with a young girl, later fictionalized as Ying-ying. It is said that the spring following the romance he took the examination in the capital but failed.

In 802 Yüan Chen was married to Wei Ts'ung (783–809, courtesy name Hui-ts'ung; she is referred to by another courtesy name, Ch'eng-chih, in Yüan Chen's works about her), daughter of Wei Hsia-ch'ing (743–806), one of the grand tutors to the crown prince.[10] It was obviously an advantageous marriage for Yüan Chen, who did not enjoy great family prestige or political influence. The marriage seems to have taken place before Yüan Chen passed the *pa-ts'ui* examination (literally, selecting the superior talent), a kind of placement examination given by the board of civil service.[11] The candidates, who were already degree holders, were tested on specific topics of current affairs, and their essays were to be written in a prescribed literary style called *p'an* (judgments). Eight candidates passed the examination in 802, among them Po Chü-i (772–846) and Yüan Chen. The latter's name was first on the list. Both were assigned as collators of texts in the palace library.[12]

For four years the two men worked in close association. A bond stronger than that of ordinary classmates or colleagues developed between the two. Even when Yüan Chen was absent from the capital for short periods, they exchanged poems composed to the same rhyme schemes. Since their positions as collators in the palace library entailed no heavy responsibilities (they were required only to make appearances twice a month), they were left with a good deal of leisure time to pursue their own pleasures and interests. It was probably during this time that Yüan Chen compiled a compendium called *Yüan's Classification of Knowledge* (*Yüan-shih lei-chuan*), taking advantage, no doubt, of the easy access he enjoyed to the written records because of his position in the palace library.[13] Working in the palace library also provided a golden opportunity for ambitious young scholars to prepare themselves for advancement in their careers.

Between the years 803 and 806, Yüan Chen and Po Chü-i prepared themselves for the final imperial examination, which was presumably monitored by the emperor himself.[14] They attempted to anticipate all possible questions concerning current national affairs, and to devise solutions to these problems. Seventy-five of these essays resulting from their preparations were preserved by Po Chü-i in his *Collected Works*.[15] In an introduction prefacing this collection of essays called *Forest of Plans* (*Ts'e-lin*), Po Chü-i testifies to their collaboration.

In the beginning of the *yüan-ho* period, when our terms as collators of texts were over, Yüan Chen and I retreated to the Hua-yang Temple in the northern ward of the capital, and shut ourselves away for months in preparation for the *ying-chih* [palace] examinations. We hypothesized and anticipated all the possible problems and overriding issues that confronted the empire at the time, and attempted to offer solutions. Our answers resulted in the *Forest of Plans* on seventy-five topics. Yüan Chen passed the examination in first position and I was next to him. But only one to two percent of the problems and solutions we had anticipated were applicable to the examination we took. Since we had expended so much energy on these essays, I could not bear to discard them. I have collected them into four *chüan* and named them *Forest of Plans*.[16]

This particular palace examination tested the candidates' breadth of knowledge as well as their literary expertise. Since Yüan Chen headed the list of eighteen successful candidates who passed in the category specified as "both talented and erudite and capable of practical application" (*Ts'ai shih chien mao ming-yü t'i-yung*), he was immediately given a post in the court as censor of the left (*tso shih-yi*).[17] There are several versions of this term in translation, but none satisfactorily conveys the nature of this post. The incumbent in this office served as a kind of personal secretary to the emperor, and he was occasionally allowed to speak his mind on state affairs and matters of policy. Moreover, it was his duty to remind the emperor on matters that had been overlooked. The censor of the left did not rank high in the bureaucracy, nor did he enjoy any specific authority in matters of policy or decisionmaking. However, he was in frequent and close contact with the emperor, and therefore in a position to influence him in matters of importance. Yüan Chen took advantage of the situation and made innovative proposals directly to the throne. In this way, he gained recognition in the eyes of the emperor, but he aroused the wrath and jealousy of those in power, men who had ways to curb his political career.

According to the traditional Confucian view, society was composed of four classes: the scholar, the farmer, the artisan, and the merchant, socially stratified in that descending order. Included in the scholarly class were not only scholars in the narrow sense of that term, but also government officials whose positions were attained mainly through Confucian learning and proficiency in the civil examinations. Aside from teaching and clerical work in the lower bureaucracy, no other profession was open to the scholar except government service; hence a successful political career became the goal of the young man privileged enough to have been given the kind of education that could qualify him for the competitive examinations. And, since the Confucian ideology was the basis of the classical education, all officials in the bureaucracy during T'ang times were supposed to share the same moral ethics, such as loyalty to the ruler, filial piety, and the observance of rituals and rules of propriety.

The early motivation that pushed Yüan Chen to apply himself in his youth to the study of the Confucian classics and to the perfection of his literary style is not difficult to imagine: the desire for political advancement. In a letter to his nephews urging them to apply themselves to study, he mentioned that it was because of his widowed mother's exhortations that he had exerted himself in that direction. Was his success prompted by the desire "to save the world," as he frequently stated, or simply to gain personal fame and fortune? The two were not irreconcilable, since the only way to make a name for oneself and to lead a life of public distinction was through an official career; and only through the official career could one serve the state and society in an effective way.

However, rather than speculating on his intentions, it would be better to examine his actions as an official to determine whether or not his political ambitions were self-oriented or altruistic in the Confucian manner, and whether or not he realized his political ambitions, to which he referred frequently and metaphorically as "blue clouds."[18]

His career was a checkered one; he was tossed up and down by the tidal waves of political instability. He reached the crest of political prominence when he was appointed chief minister in the administration. Unfortunately, his tenure in the chief ministership was less than four months.[19] Hardly before he had accustomed himself to that office, he was removed and sent once more into the provinces.

II *Personal Integrity and Public Image*

The biographies of Yüan Chen in both the *Old T'ang History* (*Chiu T'ang-shu*) and the *New T'ang History* (*Hsin T'ang-shu*) quote Yüan Chen's long memorial to the throne "On Educating the Prince," (*Lun chiao pen shu*), which he wrote shortly after he received the new appointment.[20] It is an impressive treatise, showing great erudition in the classical learning of the past, courage in speaking up against the current system, and insight into the problems of the day. The Hsien-tsung emperor was so pleased with the memorial that he granted Yüan Chen a special audience to consult with him on matters of state, such as policy concerning the northwestern territories. This favoritism only incurred the greater displeasure of Yüan Chen's enemies. When Yüan Chen submitted a "Ten Point Proposal"[21] in a lengthy memorial concerning the personal conduct of the emperor and the state of affairs in the imperial household, the chief minister, presumably Cheng Yu-ch'ing (748–820), accused him of meddling in the affairs of state and insubordination. According to Yüan Chen, both his motives and suggestions were misrepresented, and he was arrested and incarcerated for offenses against the throne.[22] Through the intervention of some ministers with similar complaints, and possibly that of the emperor himself, Yüan Chen was not imprisoned for more than a day or two. He was banished to Lo-yang to serve as a minor official. However, his mother died at this time, possibly from the shock of her son's misfortune; consequently, Yüan Chen retired from the political arena to observe the prescribed mourning period, which lasted until the spring of 809.[23]

While Yüan Chen had political enemies at court, he was not without friends. Among his supporters were P'ei Chi (765–813), who was earlier his supervisor in the palace examinations, Ling-hu Ch'u (766–837), and Li Chiang (764–830), who were all chief ministers at one time or another between more conservative administrations. When Yüan Chen came out of mourning, his patron, P'ei Chi, had become chief minister; thus it was no surprise that Yüan Chen was immediately appointed inspecting censor (*chien-ch'a yü-shih*) and entrusted to make a special inspection tour of east Szechwan (Tung-ch'uan).

Undaunted by earlier setbacks, Yüan Chen undertook his mission with great ardor, probably believing that he could rid the provinces of political corruption. At his new post he sent back to Ch'ang-an memorial after memorial listing in great detail all the crimes and corruption of the local military governor, Yen Li (who had died before Yüan's arrival), and his subordinates, demanding that Yen Li be dishonored posthumously. Those of Yen Li's associates who had influence and connections in court pressed for Yüan Chen's transfer. Consequently, he was sent to head the Tung-t'ai branch office of the censorate circuit in Lo-yang. While he was away from the capital, his wife Wei Ch'eng-chih died in the seventh month, and was buried in Hsien-yang outside of Ch'ang-an in the tenth month of 809.[24]

A more prudent person would have taken the transfer as a strong warning against his personal security. Not so Yüan Chen, who, having been made head of the Tung-t'ai branch office of the censorate circuit, began to investigate the malfeasance of Fang Shih (d. 812), the mayor of Lo-yang, who was responsible for the death of a young student. Having sent in a report exposing this local official, Yüan Chen took upon himself the responsibility of removing the culprit from office. Fang Shih appealed. Yüan Chen was recalled to the capital to face charges of overstepping his authority.[25]

On his way to the capital another incident occurred. On the surface it appears to have been entirely coincidental, but considering its repercussions on Yüan Chen's career, it could have been staged by his opponents in power. The events as officially recorded were: Yüan stopped for the night at a government hostel at Fu-shui, a half way station between Lo-yang and

Ch'ang-an. He was already in bed when the eunuch Liu Shih-yüan (*HTS* has a different name: Ch'ou Shih-liang) arrived and demanded that Yüan yield his suite (which was probably the best in the hostel).[26] When Yüan Chen refused, the eunuch broke down the door. Yüan fled in his stocking feet by the back door. The eunuch pursued him and hit him in the face with a whip. The administration put the entire blame on Yüan for not showing deference to the eunuch, who apparently had seniority over Yüan Chen, who was barely thirty at the time and of relatively low rank. As a consequence, Yüan was demoted and banished to Chiang-ling at the beginning of 810. His friend Po Chü-i, who was then a *shih-i* (personal censor) to the emperor, sent three memorials protesting the unfair treatment accorded Yüan Chen by the administration. Besides Po, two other upright, sympathetic officials, Li Chiang and Ts'ui Ch'ün (772–832), likewise sent in memorials on Yüan Chen's behalf, all to no avail.[27]

Thus, from 810 to 815 Yüan Chen, with all his grand plans of helping the people and reconstructing the nation, held a minor office of administrator of works (*Shih-ts'ao ts'an-ch'un shih*) in Chiang-ling (Ching-chou) on the middle Yangtze River. Later, in the spring of 815, he was recalled to Ch'ang-an for reassignment and was sent to T'ung-chou in Szechwan as a marshal (*szu-ma*), a slightly higher rank than the previous post. There he was to stay four more years. A few months after he was transferred to Kuo-chou as a deputy prefect in 819, he was again recalled to Ch'ang-an, and was given the title of auxiliary secretary of the board of banquets, an honorary title without any real authority.[28]

III *The Climax of a Political Career*

The Hsien-Tsung emperor's sudden death (presumably murdered by a powerful eunuch faction) ended the *yüan-ho* period. The new emperor, Mu-tsung, changed the reign title to *ch'ang-ch'ing* in 821. When the new emperor was still a prince he had frequently heard Yüan Chen's poems recited and sung by court ladies, who had dubbed the poet "Yüan the Genius" (*Yüan ts'ai-tzu*). Shortly after he ascended the throne, he was offered several hundred of Yüan Chen's poems by the eunuch Ts'ui T'an-chün, who had met the poet earlier in Chiang-ling and was greatly impressed by his talent. Among these poems was the "Lien-ch'ang Palace" (*Lien-ch'ang kung tz'u*), a long poem of 90 lines in the new *yüeh-fu* style. The emperor was delighted with Yüan's poems and asked of the poet's whereabouts. When he was informed, he immediately appointed Yüan Chen to the post of secretary of the Ministry of the Rites. Shortly thereafter Yüan Chen was put in charge of drafting royal rescripts and decrees (*chih-chih kao*) in the *Han-lin* Academy.

In this capacity Yüan Chen was able to make lasting contributions to the world of letters: although it is not generally acknowledged, he played a vital part in the so-called *ku-wen* movement (Archaic Prose Movement), traditionally attributed to the efforts of Han Yü (768–824) and Liu Tsung-yüan (773–819). Enjoying an influential position, Yüan Chen undoubtedly wished to translate his ideas into action and to exercise influence in bringing to light some of the misdeeds and corruption in the administration that were the order of the day. Because he was on good terms with Wei Hung-chien (758–804), a eunuch who headed the bureau of classified documents, it was rumored that his friendship with Wei was a ploy to rob the power of the administration and would lead to the ruination of the state. P'ei Tu (765–839), a rival loyalist who was then a military governor in Ho-tung, sent three angry memorials to the throne demanding that the situation at court be corrected. Under political pressure, the emperor removed Wei from office and assigned Yüan to the post of vice-president of the Ministry of Labor. This action by the emperor was apparently an attempt to appease his disgruntled ministers. When the rumors died down shortly thereafter, Yüan was made chief minister in 822.[29] This appointment was met with hostility, possibly because Yüan had risen too high too fast, and had not advanced up the ladder by regular stages or secured regular political support and backing.

The feud between P'ei Tu and Yüan Chen began because of their opposing attitudes on matters of political and military policy. P'ei Tu, who had successfully put down the rebel Wu Yüan-chi (783–817) in Huai-hsi in 817, was eager to achieve another victory in the campaign against Wang T'ing-ts'ou (d.

834) in the northeast, the outlying region that was the cradle of the An Lu-shan Rebellion. Yüan Chen, on the other hand, incensed by the ceaseless suffering and devastation caused by constant warfare and the unfavorable conditions under which the soldiers were forced to fight, recommended that military expeditions against the rebels be stopped. In addition, his close friend Po Chü-i and others who held the same view made similar recommendations to the emperor, suggesting that P'ei Tu be given less power in the campaign. The memorial was well documented, with detailed descriptions of the situation and the disposition of troops.[30]

P'ei Tu was summoned to the capital a month after Yüan became chief minister. Perhaps to show imperial impartiality, the emperor made P'ei Tu chief minister also, with seniority over Yüan Chen. Soon another rumor, perhaps started by Yüan's enemies, began to circulate, to the effect that Yüan Chen had hired two men to assassinate P'ei Tu. An investigation was made, and the charge was proven false. But in the process of the investigation it was revealed that Yüan Chen had indeed employed two individuals of questionable character, but for a different purpose. According to Yüan Chen, he employed them because they claimed they could plot a coup in the rebel's camp in Shen-chou in order to rescue General Niu Yüan-yi (fl. 820), who was encircled. The plan was certainly ill-conceived and unwise, and smacks of modern-day espionage. Yüan admitted his own naiveté and impetuosity, but insisted that he was motivated by his eagerness to accomplish something on his own initiative to repay the imperial favor he had received.[31] This exposure discredited and embarrassed all concerned and compromised the government, so that the emperor was forced to dismiss both P'ei Tu and Yüan Chen as chief ministers. Yüan was again banished from the capital, this time to the post of prefect of T'ung-chou in Shensi.[32]

IV *The Waning Years*

From the second half of 822 until his death in 831, Yüan Chen was kept in the provinces, with only brief visits to the capital. Never again would he influence the policies of the central government. He did however institute reforms on the local level. As prefect of T'ung-chou (822–823), he tightened up the discipline of local officers, but relaxed government controls on the inhabitants; he adopted measures to economize within the government and reduced taxation. And when he was transferred from T'ung-chou, the citizens all came out to see him off, "the young and the old, the widowers and the orphans, all cried as if they were parting from their parents. They obstructed the traffic."[33]

In the fall of 823 Yüan Chen became governor of Yüeh-chou (in modern-day Chekiang province) and was concurrently assigned the office of inspector general of Che-tung. He remained in this post for eight years, although he was recalled to Ch'ang-an temporarily for other assignments and the conferral of titles of honor (he was made president of the Ministry of State Affairs). His friend Po Chü-i was in the neighboring prefecture, Hangchow, at the time. A large number of poems were exchanged between the two after 823, a fact that seems to refute the alleged cooling off of their friendship.[34]

It was during this period that Yüan Chen collected his own manuscripts. The compilation of his collected works, *Yüan-shih ch'ang-ch'ing chi* (hereafter cited as *YSCCC*), in one hundred *chüan* was completed in the winter of 823. The following year he edited the works of his friend, Po Chü-i, the *Po-shih ch'ang-ch'ing chi* (hereafter *PSCCC*), and arranged them into fifty *chüan*, together with an introduction that was dated the tenth day of the twelfth month of the fourth year of the *ch'ang-ch'ing* period (825). Moreover, the correspondence in verse between Yüan Chen and Po Chü-i continued, as far as we know, until the last years of Yüan Chen's life.

CHAPTER 3

The Political Reformer

I Early Motivation

IN a letter written to Po Chü-i in 815, Yüan Chen reminisced
about his early life as a teenager living with relatives in the
frontier town of Feng-hsiang. These were during the last years
of the Te-tsung emperor's reign, when conditions in the empire
were at a low ebb. Confucianism remained the state ideology,
but it had to contend with the rising influences of Taoism and
Buddhism. Corruption in government was rife among court
officials and in the provinces. Regional military leaders fought
among themselves for the control of territory and the well-
being of the population received scant attention. Using tribute
to the emperor as a pretext, local officials robbed the people of
their livelihood. The further removed from the central government, the more lawlessness occurred.

Living in a frontier region, Yüan Chen had ample occasion to
witness the sufferings of the common people, who were victimized either by warfare or by political injustice at the hands of
corrupt local officials. The impact of what he saw and heard was
strong on his young mind, and he was angered and embittered.
He confessed to Po Chü-i that when he learned from history
and the classics the principles of governing, he wanted to de-
nounce all the inequities around him. It was there and then
that he vowed to dedicate himself to the amelioration of society.[1]

In his poetry Yüan Chen frequently declared his political
ambitions and expressed his dissatisfaction with the general
conditions of the time. The first opportunity for him to voice
his opinions publicly came when he participated in the official
examinations in 802 and 806. Of his examination paper written
in 802 there is no record, except that he was warned by P'ei
Chi, his examiner, to be more cautious about what he said in the

future. His paper for the palace examination of 806, however, is preserved in his *Collected Works* (*YSCCC*). This essay may be used as a valuable document for the study of his life and ideals. The essay question supposedly posed by the Hsien-tsung emperor may be summarized as follows:

Since the An Lu-shan Rebellion and its aftermath, the conditions of the empire have been deteriorating. What can be done to remedy the situation and to restore the country to its past glory? What previous errors should be corrected and what future troubles can be avoided or guarded against? Where should the power of administration be vested? If too much is delegated to those below, there are those who take advantage of me and use power for their private ends. If I adopt an authoritarian manner, then will those below become ineffectual? Yüan Ti (r. 48–32 B.C.) of the Han dynasty emphasized Confucian scholarship and his reign declined; Emperor Kuang-wu (r. 25–57 A.D.) paid great attention to his ministers and his reign was not without great turmoil. Which is the best course of action to follow, and what are the alternatives?[2]

In his answer, a long discursive essay of more than three thousand characters, Yüan Chen attempted to defend the fundamental Confucian teachings by recommending several practical reforms in government. At the outset, he stated the traditional, formal praise to the emperor for his concern for the people, indicated by the imperial desire to select the wise and able for employment in the government, and by his encouragement of honest, direct criticism. In the same breath, however, Yüan Chen questioned the sincerity of the establishment in adhering to its original intention by saying: "I do not know whether there are outspoken scholars who would respond to the call for criticism, or whether the proposals of forthright scholars ever receive the proper attention they deserve...."[3] His doubts about the government's good faith, however, did not hinder him from offering suggestions, and in recommending solutions to the problems of the day he minced no words. In essence, he attributed the cause of the nation's ills to a lack of efficiency and benevolence in the government.

In the past, after our founding emperor Wu-ti had brought order out of chaos, our former emperor T'ai-tsung laid down his arms and wrapped the empire with benevolence and generosity. With the reduction of conscription, the common people could again live in peace; with the limited use of capital punishment, many lives were spared. Since he ruled according to the will of the people, harmony prevailed; since he selected the virtuous and the wise for office, the masses were governed according to principle. When principle prevailed, there existed respect and deference. When there was harmony between the rulers and the ruled, then there was love among those who receive instructions. . . .

But after the T'ien-pao era (742–756), the military gradually took over the administration. When the military spirit waxed, moral principles waned. Those who had been nurtured in the past were then victimized by the armed forces. Ever since then militarism has become a thorny issue. With the growing strength of the military, the number of civilians is reduced. With the reduction of the civilian population, the fields lie in waste. With the fields lying in waste, taxation becomes exorbitant. With exorbitant taxation, the masses become impoverished. With the masses impoverished, the number of draft dodgers and tax evaders is on the increase. With increasing numbers of criminals engaging in draft dodging and tax evasion, there are more punishments and restrictions. . . .

It is my humble opinion that in order to revive the [ancient] teachings of rites and music, the common people must first be free from want. So that the people may be free from want, we must put a stop to the expansion of the armed forces by reducing military spending.

I would like to speak of a reduction in military spending and of curbs on the further growth of the armed forces. This is what the ancient sages spoke of as "disarmament." This, however, does not literally mean to tear up the military banners or to melt down weapons. If those in high positions could manifest their credibility and good faith, there would be loyalty and filial piety from those below. If within the empire there is prosperity and the expectancy of long life, then barbarian tribes outside the country will live in peace and harmony. If barbarian tribes could live in peace and harmony, then there will be no military conflict on the frontiers. If life and prosperity are established, then the fear of strife and aggression will disappear and harmony and submission will ensue. Only when there is submission in man's heart can the rites and music prevail. This is the general outline of how the ancient kings used their administrations to cease hostilities and to enrich the people with the teachings of the sages on the rites and music.[4]

II *On the Examination System*

On his list of reform priorities, Yüan Chen in the same examination essay recommended changes in the examination system. On this issue he proposed the selection of public officials exclusively through the civil service examinations. The civil service examination system was an old institution that had come into existence during the Han dynasty. But it fell into disuse for centuries, until the Sui dynasty reintroduced it as a means of selecting public officials. The T'ang examination system differed from earlier models in that it emphasized written examinations as a way to determine a candidate's competency, whereas during early times selections were based mainly on recommendations by local leaders and government officials.

Although the examinations carried greater weight than before in appointments to office, recommendations and hereditary honors remained contributing elements in the candidate's success or failure, and, in certain instances, the examinations could be waived for those who held special privileges. During Yüan Chen's own time, the selection of candidates depended heavily upon the recommendations of incumbent government officials. In principle, the system allowed all talented men in the empire to participate, regardless of family background or origin. In practice, however, many people of the lower social strata were barred from participation; those with influential family backgrounds received preferential treatment. Moreover, the successful candidates for the coveted degrees were frequently experts only in literary matters and not necessarily competent in administration. When these people were appointed to official posts, they were likely to fail.

"The trouble with the current examination system," claimed Yüan Chen, "is that it is antiquated." The holders of the "clarification of the classics" degree, for instance, could recite the classics without really understanding the meaning of the ancient texts: "Thus every year hundreds pass the examination, but few really understand the true teachings of the classics ... while those who excel in letters are only talented in the use of words and versification, but have little knowledge of the art of governing. Moreover, some of the people who are selected by the court are not known for any talent. . . ."[5]

To remedy all of these shortcomings, Yüan Chen proposed that changes be made in the regulations governing the civil service examinations. First of all, he argued, the examinations should be open to everyone, even those of the humblest birth, and not exclusively to those of the hereditary official class. He also advocated the maintenance of the two categories in the examinations given by the board of rites. In one category the candidates were to be examined on the rites, the constitution, and the history of the T'ang dynasty; in the other, they were to be tested for their literary accomplishments, such as writing in the *fu* and *p'an* genres.[6] Instead of a further placing examination, which could be eliminated, appointments should be given according to the results of these initial examinations; promotions and demotions would be based on actual performance on the job. Unfortunately, none of these innovative proposals were adopted.

III *On the Education of the Prince*

After Yüan Chen was given an official post in the chancellery as a censor (*tso shih-yi*), his first official act was to submit a memorial in fifteen hundred words (written, no doubt, on the special official paper used on these occasions) concerning the education of the prince: "On the Education of the Prince" (*Lun chiao-pen shu*). The proper education of the crown prince, he argued in the memorial, was insurance of an enlightened ruler and an enlightened government. Drawing upon ancient history, Yüan Chen pointed out that, even during the legendary Three Dynasties, all those humane and wise rulers were not born so, but became "sage kings" through proper education. "King Ch'eng of Chou, for instance, was of average intelligence. When he was close to Kuan and Ts'ai (wicked ministers), he was susceptible to flattery and slander. But when he had Chou and Shao (loyal ministers), then his righteousness was known."[7]

Yüan Chen later elaborated on the reasons why King Ch'eng could follow the ways of the ancients: he was raised in the proper environment and assisted by wise tutors and righteous men, such as the Duke of Chou and the Duke of Shao. With beneficial influences all around him, he was not corrupted by wicked attendants to seduce him to such pleasures as chasing birds and beasts, so that he had ample time for serious studies. After citing several examples of how good rulers were educated through proper training and guidance by wise tutors, Yüan Chen went on to speculate on the cause of the downfall of the Ch'in dynasty (221–206 B.C.)

To foster ignorance in the world, the Ch'in dynasty destroyed the Confucian classics handed down by the ancient kings. How could they [the House of Ch'in] then have wise and enlightened tutors to guide their princes? The heir of Ch'in, Hu Hai (r. 209–207 B. C.), had no opportunity to hear about the classics, nor the opportunity to be near the wise and the virtuous. The treacherous eunuch Chao Kao (d. 207 B.C.) could only teach him the skills of killing people and terrorizing the world . . . although the entire empire did not become ignorant, Hu Hai himself was unable to distinguish wild from domestic animals. Chao Kao's power intimidated the whole empire, and Hu Hai, confined in the palace, was the eunuch's prisoner. Li Ssu (280?–208 B.C.) was the favorite prime minister of the Ch'in regime, but he had no way to clear himself of all the slanders and charges against him. Much less could other ministers, who had been long alienated by Chao Kao from the throne, come to his assistance. Consequently, the destruction of Ch'in was inevitable.[8]

After presenting a brief historical review of Han times, when the teachings of Confucianism were reestablished, thus diverting the course of a downward trend, Yüan returned to his main theme:

During the reign of our own emperor T'ai-tsung, when Kao-tsung was still the crown prince, eighteen men of virtue were selected to accompany him constantly at study and at play. After he came to the throne, there were people similar to those eighteen virtuous men attending him at meals or at recreation. They would remonstrate if there was anything remiss on the part of the emperor. Within four years, the emperor's reputation as a sage-ruler spread. Such results could not be accomplished in a day or two; it was through constant vigilance and education.[9]

In the final section of the memorial, he points out that the important mission of training the crown prince was gradually neglected. Posts of imperial tutors came to be filled by incompetent, old, or disabled officials, or even by retired generals lacking any real learning; and the companions to the prince were mostly a base, indolent, fawning lot. "Even the commoners who love their sons," claimed Yüan Chen, "would seek the enlightened, the intelligent, the virtuous to be their sons' teachers; the straightforward, the well-informed, to be their sons' companions." In the main, his proposal was that the emperor should exercise special care in selecting qualified scholars of high moral integrity to be in charge of the crown prince's education, and that all other princes be allowed to be educated by the same tutors. In this way, when the crown prince came to the throne he could select the best among his blood relations to guard the provinces. Yüan Chen concluded the memorial by saying: "What a difference this would be when compared with those regimes since Wei and Chin, when brothers were at each other's throats, and when it was as if one were to cut down one's own roots and branches."[10]

Some critics have concluded that Yüan Chen was hasty in presenting his ideas to the throne on the education of the crown princes, and that this was mainly an attempt to attract attention to his own person. If that were so, he could have chosen to take a milder and safer course. Instead, in discussing the manner in which the crown prince was being groomed for the throne, he must have antagonized more than those in the employ of the Southern Palace (i.e., the headquarters of the crown prince, who usually lived separately from the rest of the princes). His reference to the infamous eunuch Chao Kao and the young puppet ruler, Hu Hai, of the Ch'in dynasty could very well have been construed as an indirect attack on the powerful eunuchs at court who had assisted Hsien-tsung in gaining the throne. Fortunately, Hsien-tsung was impressed rather than insulted by Yüan Chen's long memorial. There was, however, no indication that any of Yüan Chen's advice was taken seriously, although we do know that Yüan Chen was later summoned to audience on several occasions and was consulted on frontier problems at Huai-hsi.[11]

IV   *The "Ten Point Proposal"*

Encouraged by the favor the emperor had shown him, and eager to bring about envisioned reforms, Yüan Chen sent forward another long memorial, this one even more critical of court officials for shirking their duty to offer plans and suggestions for the improvement of the state administration. Citing a series of historical examples about former rulers who listened to frank criticism and accepted suggestions from the daring and loyal ministers, so that others would take courage and dare to assist them to right wrongs, he stated bluntly: "If a ruler appears deaf or blind, it is not that he is without ears or eyes. Only those around him prevent him from hearing or seeing . . . , for surely everyone likes obedience and flattery and is offended by frank criticism and remonstrance. However, one must weigh the consequences between the pleasure of the moment and the lasting peace of the empire. . . ." After a scathing stricture against those who, out of fear, refrained from giving sound suggestions, Yüan Chen offered his own "Ten Point Proposal":

(1)   Educate the crown prince in such a way as to stabilize the foundations of the empire.

(2)   Provide administrative duties for younger brothers of the emperor in order to consolidate the strength of the imperial house.

(3)   Reduce the imperial harem in order to balance the *yin* and *yang* forces of nature and thereby avoid flood and drought (which are manifestations of imbalances in nature).

(4)   Allow palace ladies to marry in order to fulfill human nature.

(5)   Hold conferences constantly with ministers to discuss affairs of state.

(6)   Give audience to other officials to gain broader perspectives and understanding.

(7)   Revive the practice of accepting memorials at court levees.

(8)   Allow impeachment concerning the wrongdoings of officials and conduct investigations into their alleged crimes.

(9)   Forbid gifts and tributes to the emperor, except on prescribed occasions, so as to forestall demands for imperial favors.

(10) Reduce the number of imperial hunting expeditions in order to prevent possible accident.[12]

V *Yüan's Antiwar Attitudes*

Like most Confucian scholars, Yüan Chen did not believe in military solutions to social or political problems. His general attitude toward war and military conflict, as indicated in many of his poems, clashed with that of the Hsien-tsung emperor, during whose reign Yüan's own political career began. Hsien-tsung took a hard line aginst the separatists who were claiming independence in the provinces and refusing to send tribute to the central government. Since the country was still trying to recover from the devastating aftermath of the An Lu-shan Rebellion, the extensive and prolonged military campaigns ordered by Hsien-tsung only added to the hardship, resentment, and rebelliousness of the common people. Yüan Chen's attitude toward war was Confucian in outlook and persuasion. According to Confucian theory, recourse to military means was proof of failure on the part of the ruler to provide the kind of government under which the people could live in peace and harmony. If the country was at peace within, it would command respect without, and the barbarian tribes beyond the frontiers would not create disturbances but would live in mutual respect and harmony with the Chinese. It was assumed that only a corrupt government could be infested by civil wars and foreign invasions. The policy of seeking military solutions was like trying to cure an infection without treating the cause.

Undoubtedly Yüan Chen was not alone in this view—many of his friends and colleagues shared this attitude, especially those of humbler origin who had witnessed the effects of war on the common people or had shared the suffering that resulted from constant warfare. They all believed that those in court who advocated military solutions were not concerned for the interests of the people; especially among the eunuchs, war provided opportunities for self-advancement and personal gain. The advocates of war, on the other hand, usually mobilized support in the name of honor, loyalty, and patriotism. Debate on these issues among the ministers at court must have been in some ways comparable to that between the so-called "hawks" and "doves" in recent discussions on American foreign policy.

If Yüan Chen was not consistent in his personal conduct or in

his party affiliations, as some historians have suggested, he was
certainly consistent in his views on militarism. His failure to come
to prominence during Hsien-tsung's reign and his inability to hold
on to his ministership during Mu-tsung's reign could both have
been due chiefly to his antiwar attitudes. But to call his a
pacifist's attitude or a natural aversion to war may be mis-
leading, because in some of his poems he does praise government military victories. He was not against all wars so much as
he was opposed to human suffering as a result of war. More
fundamentally, he was against the fundamental causes that make
war necessary. He wanted to see certain reforms carried out
by the central government administration and reflected in the
personal conduct and behavior of its officials. If wise and
benevolent rule prevailed, he believed, the necessity for war
and punitive measures against rebels would be removed. Thus,
besides being a political moderate, he was also a reformist committed to cleaning up governmental corruption wherever it
occurred.

VI *War Against Corruption*

While many high officials in court disliked Yüan Chen immensely for what he believed as well as for his impetuous
character and intrepid behavior, there must have been some,
specifically P'ei Chi and Ling-hu Ch'u (both chief ministers at
different times) who wanted to see his innate uprightness and
sense of justice utilized for the good of the state. Thus, in 809,
when he emerged from the prescribed period of mourning for
his mother, Yüan Chen was named imperial inspecting censor
and sent on special mission to Tung-ch'uan (modern eastern
Szechwan province), where rumors of official corruption called
for an investigation. There he found ample evidence of
corruption.

The principal culprit, Yen Li, the military governor of Chien-
nan East, had died shortly before Yüan's arrival in the third
lunar month of 809. His misdeeds and those of his subordinates,
however, were exposed by Yüan Chen. In a long memorial impeaching Yen Li, Yüan Chen documented his crimes item by
item, including exact dates and names. An English version of this

memorial is found in Charles Peterson's article, "Corruption Unmasked: Yüan Chen's Investigations in Szechwan."[13] Briefly, Yen was accused of such abuses of power as illegal confiscation of private lands, properties, and servants of hundreds of families on trumped-up charges of aiding and abetting the rebels; imposition of taxes and levies on the lands and people under his administration without authorization from the central government; withholding military supplies and soldiers' pay; and misappropriation of grain, silk, and fodder from several prefectures under his governance.[14] After summing up Yen's crimes and those of his subordinates with individual listing, Yüan Chen recommended that Yen Li, though dead, be posthumously dishonored and that all honorary titles conferred upon him earlier be withdrawn, so that others would be forewarned from committing similar crimes. Yen's subordinates who either colluded with Yen or violated the laws on their own should all be severely disciplined.[15]

It seems that Yen Li and his subordinates must have had strong backing in the imperial court, presumably from powerful eunuchs who, at one time or another, had served as liaison officers between the emperor and the military governors. The great effort Yüan Chen expended in the investigation of this case, however, bore little fruit. While some restitution was made to Yen's victims, Yen Li was not posthumously dishonored, as Yüan Chen had suggested, and his cohorts escaped punishment. They were fined two days' salary, and the case was closed. Yüan Chen, on the other hand, had much to lose: as a result of this investigation, he became the target of concerted retaliation. Instead of being returned to the imperial censorate in Ch'ang-an, he was dispatched to Tung-t'ai in Honan to open a branch office of the censorate.

Undaunted by this political setback, Yüan Chen continued in his reformist role as an investigator with undiminished zeal, exposing more miscarriages of justice under his jurisdiction. During the last month of 809, he prosecuted Han Kao, an imperial inspector and concurrently governor of Yün-chou, for having ordered Sun Chien, the magistrate of An Chi, flogged so severely that the latter died three days later. Yüan Chen concluded that in this case the punishment had far exceeded the crime, and that Han Kao had concealed the true cause of the victim's death in his report.[16]

Yüan Chen exposed other irregularities in the local government. For instance, when a eunuch military superintendent died, a governor (Wang Shao) issued illegal permits for the transportation of the coffin and a host of retainers at government expense.[17] The most serious case that Yüan Chen investigated in Tung-t'ai involved Fang Shih, mayor of Lo-yang.[18] Fang Shih had hounded a student with slander and contumely until the young man committed suicide. Yüan Chen, having discovered this and possibly other wrongdoings, removed Fang Shih from office without first consulting the court. Fang Shih appealed and was restored to his post, with a fine of only a month's salary. Yüan Chen, on the other hand, was reprimanded for overstepping his function. Besides being fined four months of his salary, he was ordered to return to Ch'ang-an for interrogation. On his way back, he had an altercation with a eunuch in a government lodging. Partly as a consequence of his handling of the Fang Shih case and partly because of the incident with the eunuch (which may well have been staged by Yüan's enemies), Yüan Chen was demoted and banished from court for the second time, and this time for ten years.

Yüan Chen's impeachments of local officials and his unfair treatment are substantiated by Po Chü-i's memorials protesting his friend's banishment as a result of those actions. Po wrote three such memorials, but only the third is extant. Other officials, such as Li Chiang and Ts'ui Ch'ün, also memorialized the throne on Yüan Chen's behalf. In his extant memorial, Po Chü-i accused the emperor of injustice in banishing Yüan Chen and gave three reasons to substantiate his argument.[19] The emperor was not swayed by Po Chü-i's argument—Yüan Chen was not recalled immediately from banishment as Po had pleaded.

Ten years in exile may have damped Yüan Chen's youthful reformist spirit, but it did not bring to an end his ambition to serve whenever and wherever he could.[20] If as a result of these experiences the young idealist became in time a practical man, it was because he had been victimized by the system. One can never know for sure whether, had he held the office of chief minister longer, he would have tried to put into effect some of the ideas he had espoused in his youth. If he was not as successful in carving out political reforms as he had envisioned in his youth, he was successful in some literary reforms, one of which had political significance—while heading the *Han-lin* Academy, he was responsible for changes in the language and style of imperial documents, which, in turn, escalated the so-called "archaic prose movement" (*ku-wen yün-tung*).

CHAPTER 4

The Literary Innovator

EZRA Pound, in "How to Read," classifies writers into six categories, the first two of which are the inventors and the masters.[1] According to Pound, the "inventors" are those who discover certain processes and modes of writing; the "masters" are those who can assimilate and coordinate the inventions of others and bring out something homogeneous and yet with some special quality or character of their own.[2] Yüan Chen certainly could qualify for both by the feat of his literary innovations. To place Yüan Chen as a poet and as a man in proper historical perspective, a brief survey of the literary landscape of his time is necessary. For no one is completely free from the impact of the age in which he lives—he either acts according to, or reacts against, his own environment in time and space, thereby setting a new trend, or trends, for others to follow or to reject.

I Literary Reforms

One cannot survey T'ang dynasty literary trends without mentioning some of the literary reforms that marked the process of change in a dynamic, living literature. The most prominent of the various literary reforms is known as the *ku-wen* movement (literally, "ancient prose").[3] This movement called for a return to antiquity in prose styles, especially the style of the Han and pre-Han eras that characterizes the Confucian classics. Primarily this movement was a reaction against the prevalent literary trend of "parallel prose" (*p'ien-wen*—literally, "harnessed prose"), a prose style that required an ornate and florid diction, an excessive use of antitheses and parallelism, and contrived sentence structures and end rhymes.[4] Stemming from the literary genre of *fu*, this so-called "parallel prose" came into vogue during the latter part of the Six Dynasties (222–589).[5]

44

During T'ang times, it was so widely employed that even official government communications had adopted such modes of writing. As a result, the true function of language was largely ignored; and the overemphasis on literary formalism and aesthetic considerations tended to enfeeble the effectiveness and clarity of communication.

Isolated efforts to bring about changes in the situation had been made previously. For instance, Su Ch'o (498–546) had drafted an edict for T'ai-tsu, the founder of the Western Wei dynasty, in the style of the *Book of History* (*Shu ching*), which signaled the first attempt to counter the pervasive influence of "parallel prose."[6] Likewise, during the Sui dynasty, Li O (fl. late sixth century) protested the literary as well as moral "decadence" of his day and memorialized the emperor, Wen-ti (r. 589–605), proposing stylistic reforms in official documents as the initial step toward eliminating chaos and confusion in government.[7] However, it was not until mid-T'ang times that a concerted attempt by scholars and officials secured sufficient support to effect appreciable changes in the writing of prose. In place of the highly artificial parallel sentence structures, the advocates of the *ku-wen* movement proposed the adoption of a simple and straightforward prose style based on Han and pre-Han texts.

Besides the language and stylistic changes, the leaders of this movement were also concerned with the moral content of literature. To raise the moral standards of their age, they advocated a "return to antiquity" (*fu-ku*), and a revival or intensification of the teachings imbedded in the Confucian classics. Form and content (i.e., "vehicle and tenor") must reinforce each other; hence their slogan: "Let literature be the vehicle of the *Tao* (i.e., the moral principle of the norm)." Traditionally, the acknowledged leaders of this movement were Han Yü and Liu Tsung-yüan, whose essays are generally regarded as practical exemplifications of the theories that generated the movement. However, others also contributed significantly to its success, among them Yüan Chen. Two major factors that enhanced the success of the movement were: (1) official sanctions of the adoption of classical prose style, which came to be known as the "new" prose style;[8] (2) the birth of a literary genre, *ch'uan-*

ch'i ("transmission of the marvelous") written in a straightforward style free from the affectations of contrived parallelism and excessive allusiveness. In both areas Yüan Chen was to make important personal contributions.

II *Personal Contributions*

The *ku-wen* movement began to take shape during the last years of the *chen-yüan* era (785–805) and flourished during the *yüan-ho* period (806–821), a time roughly corresponding to Yüan Chen's most productive years. His contributions to the movement, which have never been fully acknowledged, may be summarized as follows: (1) the use of a simple and clear literary style in his novella (*ch'uan-ch'i*), "The Story of Ying-ying" (*"Ying-ying chuan"*; also known as *"Hui-chen chi"*);[9] (2) the incorporation of the basic tenets of the *ku-wen* movement, the ethical and utilitarian functions of literature, in his own critical theories; and most importantly, (3) the promotion of the classical prose style in the drafting of imperial rescripts when he headed the *Han-lin* Academy.

A casual perusal of Yüan Chen's *Collected Works* (*YSCCC*) shows that hardly any of his early prose writings belong to the "parallel prose" that was in vogue, although occasional use was made of parallel structures. The most famous of his prose writings is unquestionably "The Story of Ying-ying," which has had a lasting and indelible literary influence on later Chinese literature.[10] Stylistically, it is one of the most successful pieces of prose fiction written in the T'ang dynasty. Most critics agree that this work surpasses by far the prose fiction, "The Biography of Mao Ying" (*"Mao Ying chuan"*), written by Han Yü.[11] Not only is the language of the former charged with a greater emotional intensity than that of the latter, but Yüan Chen found a way to explore the full potentials of this new, literary prose style, which in turn helped to popularize the rather esoteric *ku-wen* movement.

Yüan Chen's most effective contribution to the success of this movement came later, however. It was only during Mu-tsung's reign (821–825) that he undertook to drastically reform the written style of official rescripts as a matter of public policy.

His own prose works exemplify the classical style he advocated, of which 144 pieces are still extant. They range from his draft of imperial decrees covering public pardons, eulogies on ministers' duties well-performed, and invocations to be read at the imperial ancestral temple. In an introduction to his collection of rescripts, which comprise eleven *chüan* in his *Collected Works*, Yüan Chen gives his own justification for the need of literary reform:

Rescripts have their sources in the *Book of History* [*Shu ching*, one of the five Confucian classics]. The proclamations, decrees, injunctions, and oaths in the *Shu* were issued for restraint and discipline at given moments. Since they were for the purpose of giving instruction or guidance, it would seem necessary to express clearly what was good and what was bad, so that rewards and punishments could be dealt out accordingly. Thus, when we read the "Command of Fu Yüeh" [*Yüeh ming*],[12] we know how difficult a task it is to conduct oneself as a helpful minister. Only after reading "The Punitive Expedition of Prince Yin" [*Yin cheng*] do we realize how laziness and remission deserve punishment.[13] It [this fundamental principle] has not been altered since Ch'in and Han times. But more recently in our own times, the officials selected by the examination system to execute written communications have become engrossed in decorative literary expression at the expense of matter and substance. Their language may be overflowing with extollment, but one cannot discern what is being extolled. A written dismissal is full of blame, but the source of the blame is not made known. Moreover, the writing is fettered by parallelism and cramped into set molds of circles and squares, comparable to the *fu* and *p'an* genres.[14] The original intention of the ancient kings to discipline and restrain is cast aside and dashed to the ground.[15]

In the same introduction Yüan Chen also tells us how he effected stylistic changes in the drafting of rescripts. He recalls that in 820, while he was serving as assistant secretary in the Ministry of Rites, he had already raised objections to the use of parallel prose as the official style of writing, and had expressed his opinion to one of the chief ministers, who seemed to agree with him. However, nothing came of his suggestions until the following year, when he was made head of the *Han-lin* Academy, which had the responsibility to draft or supervise the drafting of imperial documents. In this capacity he was in close proximity to the emperor and able to offer his proposals directly. "The emperor was very fond of letters. . . . One day we discussed the matter of style at length. His Majesty decreed that writing was for the purpose of communication. . . . Since then, all those whose official function it is to write were charged to follow the ways of the ancients and not emulate the styles of the decadent period [of the more recent past]."[16]

Following the ways of the ancients meant simplicity of diction, clarity of expression, and sincerity of thought and content. In essence, Yüan Chen adhered to the fundamental tenets associated with the *ku-wen* movement concerning both form and content. Yüan Chen did not call for a return to the ancient style alone; he devoted equal attention to content. This is demonstrated by his emphasis on the study of the Confucian classics as exemplary models of the ethical and moral concerns of the ancient sages—aesthetic considerations became secondary in importance in the face of ethical and moral questions, which must be the primary concern of a good government. Sincerity of language reflects sincerity of thought and vice versa. This idea of interrelatedness between thought and action, however, was not unique with Yüan Chen. Even today, many writers still believe that verbal expression is but an external manifestation of thought, and as such it is also symptomatic of the mental health of the individual. No wonder Yüan Chen, the Confucian idealist, should have been acridly critical of a "decadent" prose style that overemphasized linguistic niceties and technical refinements but ignored the real function of language, namely, communication.

If Yüan Chen's contribution to the *ku-wen* movement has not been generally recognized by posterity, it was, however, duly acknowledged by the historians who compiled both the *Old T'ang History* and the *New T'ang History*. The former mentions that Yüan Chen's own style was "eminently superior, even comparable to the classics of the ancients, so that it had become highly admired during the period"; the latter states that Yüan Chen "changed the written style of the rescripts, emphasizing simplicity, clarity, and sincerity."[17]

III *The Four Stages of T'ang Poetry*

Most Chinese literary historians tend to divide the literary history of the T'ang dynasty into periods. Yen Yü (fl. 1180–1235) of the Sung dynasty, in his *Ts'ang-lang shih-hua*, divided T'ang poets into three categories according to their dates: i.e., poets of the Early T'ang, poets of the Mid-T'ang, and poets of the Late T'ang.[18] He confessed, however, that some of the poets he placed in the second group could very well belong to the first, and some to the last, in their literary tendencies.[19] Kao Ping (1350–1423) of the Ming dynasty made a more clear-cut division of T'ang poetry, this time into four periods, marked by the beginnings and ends of reign periods: (1) the Early T'ang, from the founding of the T'ang empire to the *yen-ho* period (608–712); (2) High T'ang, from the beginning to the end of Hsüan-tsung's reign (713–755); (3) Mid-T'ang, from the beginning of Su-tsung's reign to the end of the *t'ai-ho* period (756–835); and (4) Late T'ang, from the beginning of the *k'ai-ch'eng* period of Wen-tsung's reign (827–840) to the end of the T'ang dynasty (836–906).[20] This is generally followed by Chinese writers today with slight modifications.

The process of change in Chinese poetry, or, indeed, in any other literary development, is dynamic and fluid and not subject to arbitrary periodic demarcations. Any system of division is a matter of convenience; at best it can only highlight the most obvious characteristics of certain eras, eschewing the overlapping gray areas in which evolutionary tendencies are not yet clear or complete. In essence, the poetry of Early T'ang was simply an extension of the literary trends of the preceding age. That is to say, poets continued to develop the legacies of the court poetry of the Southern and Northern dynasties—in particular, the prosodic rules established by Shen Yüeh (441–513) and Yü Hsin (fl. sixth century A.D.). The representative poets of this period were Shen Ch'üan-ch'i (650–713?), Sung Chih-wen (ca. 660–712), Chang Chiu-ling (673–740), and Ch'en Tzu-ang (661–702). The first pair were restricted by the rules of parallelism inherited from the poets of the Liang and Ch'i dynasties; the second pair, reacting against this prevalent trend, consciously imitated earlier poets of the Wei and Chin dynasties. If attempts at innovation were made by early T'ang poets, it was not until several decades later that any degree of maturity was reached.

The second period (High or Prosperous T'ang) must be considered by any standard to represent the apogee of T'ang poetry, since the most celebrated of Chinese poets, Li Po (701–762) and Tu Fu (712–770), both belong to this period. The prosodic rules of the "new style" poetry experimented with by poets of the Early T'ang had now been mastered. A transformation had taken place in versification. Instead of brittle, raw forms, they had become pliable in the hands of poets who could use the highly restrictive patterns as naturally as ordinary speech. In terms of verbal expression, the poets of this period were endowed with greater imagination and vision, due in no small part to the social conditions both prior to and after the An Lu-shan Rebellion. Like barometers of the age, these poets signaled with great sensitivity and intensity the impending storm. Li Po and Tu Fu were not the only successful poets of this period. Stylistically, Wang Ch'ang-ling (?–756) and Wang Han (675?–746?) successfully mastered the seven character quatrain (ch'i-chüeh), while Wang Wei (699–759) and Meng Hao-jan (689–740) were more successful in advancing the development of the five character verse form (wu-lü).

The third period (Mid-T'ang), to which Yüan Chen and his friend Po Chü-i belonged, was perhaps the most complex and vital in literary activity. The poets of this period grew up in the shadow of the literary giants, Li Po and Tu Fu, and experienced the political disorder and social unrest following the An Lu-shan Rebellion. But they benefited from their predecessors' successes in perfecting the new poetic patterns and prosodic rules, in that they could concentrate on developing their own special creative talents. Although the socially oriented Yüan-Po school (Yüan Chen and Po Chü-i) was most representative of this period, there were others, such as the nature poets Wei Ying-wu (737–790?) and Liu Tsung-yüan, who wrote after the fashion of Wang Wei and Meng Hao-jan. In versification, while Liu Yü-hsi (772–842) and Chang Chi (ca. 780–850) consciously emulated the quatrain form as perfected by Li Po, Han Yü, Li Ho (791–817), and Meng Chiao (751–814) departed from that norm and developed a poetic style that was both baroque and arcane in imagery and in diction. Theirs could have been a natural reaction against the popularity of the unadorned and facile style of Yüan Chen and Po Chü-i, which dominated the *yüan-ho* period.

Likewise, the poetry of the fourth period (Late T'ang) can in some respects be considered a polar opposite in form and content to the poetry of Yüan Chen and his circle. For poets belonging to the Late T'ang, e.g., Tu Mu (803–852) and Li Shang-yin (813?–858), are noted for their preciosity, verbal niceties, obscure allusions, and obsession with aesthetic considerations, the very stylistic features that Yüan Chen and his friends tried to avoid in their own poetry.

More recently, John Wu has used the seasonal terms of spring, summer, autumn, and winter to correspond symbolically to the four stages of T'ang poetry described above.[21] Note, however, the different periods in which he places Li Po and Tu Fu in his statement: "The Spring period includes the earliest T'ang bards and Wang Wei and Li Po. The Summer period includes Tu Fu and some poets who wrote about war. The Autumn period includes Po Chü-i and his circle, and Han Yü and his circle. Winter period includes Li Shang-yin, Tu Mu, Wen T'ing-yün, Hsü Hun, Lo Yin, Han Wu, and many other minor poets."[22]

It is interesting to observe that while this schema deviates from the traditional view by assigning Li Po and Tu Fu to two different periods ("Spring" and "Summer") of T'ang poetry, he maintains the traditional view by delegating to Po Chü-i and Han Yü the leading roles in the "Autumn period." Although Li Po and Tu Fu represented two quite different tendencies in T'ang poetry, each belonged to the same age. As such, they should not be separated as if they belonged to two different stages of development. Li Po, steeped in Taoism, showed a strong tendency toward romanticism in his poetry, whereas Tu Fu, the loyal Confucianist, demonstrated an equally strong tendency toward realism in his. Each in his own fashion set a trend; thus two separate literary traditions would flourish and develop for centuries to come, with sometimes one and sometimes the other in a more prominent position from age to age. Of the two main poetic circles of the Mid-T'ang ("Autumn

period") mentioned by John Wu, Po Chü-i's circle followed the
direction pointed out by Tu Fu's altruistic, social orientation,
while Han Yü's circle shared the literary legacy of Li Po in
its fondness for exotic imagery and diction. The poetry of the
Yüan-Po school was in effect more popular during that era than
that of Han Yü's circle, mainly because it was more easily understood and therefore more widely admired. Han Yü's poetry,
which is noted for its obscure imagery and difficult language,
had some followers during his own lifetime, but it had greater
influence on the poetry of the succeeding era, specifically the
poetry of Tu Mu and Li Shang-yin. These poets of the Late
T'ang consciously rejected the new style of poetry that the
Yüan-Po school had sought to establish.

IV *Poetic Innovation*

The new style of poetry initiated by Yüan Chen and Po Chü-i
was particularly in vogue and widely imitated during the *yüan-
ho* period. Consequently, it was known in the history of Chinese
literature as the *yüan-ho* style of poetry (*yüan-ho t'i*), a term
widely adopted but not fully understood or clearly defined.
Later critics have tended to apply it to all the poetic styles of
Yüan Chen and Po Chü-i, as well as to imitations of their particular styles. In a letter to Ling-hu Ch'u, Yüan Chen stated
his personal goals for poetry and provided his own explanation
of the *yüan-ho* style:

It had been more than ten years since my demotion from the imperial
censorate. During this long lull in activity, I have devoted myself
to versification, and as a result I have accumulated over a thousand
poems. Many of these poems were written with the strongest emotional intensity and with blunt, unminced words after the satirical
tradition of the *Book of Poetry* (*Shih-ching*). Some of these poems
I am even fearful of divulging to the world. Others, composed at
intervals with the wine cup, are light and trivial verses of no great
significance except for self-expression and indulgence. The latter
belong to the category of the regulated verse form which are restrictive with no exceptional merit. Unless they have definite characteristics and originality in the use of language, they easily sink into the
commonplace. It was my hope to embody in my poems profound

meaning in simple language, to invent new rhymes and rhythms, to create flawless parallelism without sacrificing the sense and feeling. However, I fear I have not been able to attain that goal. Many neophytes in the country, not realizing that a mastery of writing must be built from the foundation up, tried to imitate my style but failed to grasp the essence; as a result they produced irrelevant, shallow verses which are also passed as poems in the *yüan-ho* style.[23]

The *yüan-ho* style, so-called because of its extreme popularity during the *yüan-ho* period, was loosely categorized by Yüan Chen as "regulated poetry" (*lü shih*) which, however, is not confined to the conventional eight lines, but ranges from eight lines to several hundred lines in length. The conventional prosodic features of "regulated verse" were observed, but also with a unique feature of his own known as *tz'u-yün* (i.e., the end rhymes follow a prescribed sequence).[24]

The term *yüan-ho* style poetry was also used interchangeably with the term Yüan-Po school verse, because the style originated in the poetry these two friends wrote to harmonize with each other's verse. The particular use of *tz'u-yün*, however, was devised by Yüan Chen, and called for the second party to use the identical words for end rhymes in the precise sequence in which they appeared in the original poem. The use of prescribed rhyme words in exchange poems of this kind was not new, but the use of rhyme words in the exact order prescribed by the original poem was a new and taxing challenge, and the difficulty mounted in proportion to the length of the poem. According to Yüan Chen, he invented this demanding novelty at which he excelled in order to stump Po Chü-i, whose poetic talents otherwise rivaled his own.[25] Po Chü-i, in his letter to Yüan Chen dated 828, tends to corroborate Yüan Chen's statement. At least in the use of *tz'u-yün*, Po Chü-i admitted that he was not Yüan's equal: "Your strong point as a writer ... is that even where hampered by the rules and restrictions of the most constricting literary forms, you always manage to say exactly what you want to say, and you know well enough that I have no such gift. ... Your intention in sending these poems was clearly to get me into a tight corner and show once and for all which of us is the master."[26] However, as these original poems of Yüan Chen to which Po Chü-i referred in his letter have all been lost, it is difficult to determine whether or not Po Chü-i complied with the exacting demands of *tz'u-yün* in his responses to those poems.

The popularity of their poetry can be attested to in Yüan Chen's own words. In his preface to the first series of Po Chü-i's *Collected Works,* which bears the title *Po-shih Ch'ang-ch'ing chi* (*PSCCC*), Yüan Chen mentions that Po Chü-i's and his own poems were to be found everywhere: "They are scribbled on the walls of palace buildings, temples, and post stations; they are recited by princes, nobles, and their consorts, and also by un-educated old women and young girls, even by cowherds and stable boys. In fact they are copied, printed, and sold in market-places, and swapped for wine or tea. This has occurred in many regions."[27] He added in a note that this was particularly true in the districts of Yang-chou and Yüeh-chou, where not only their style was copied, but their names were forged on spurious works to increase their market value.[28] In the same preface he speaks of a time when he went to P'ing-shui, a small market town near Mirror Lake (in the prefecture of Yang-chou), and noticed that the school children in the village were reciting poetry. Upon inquiry, the children proudly told him that their teacher had taught them poems by Yüan Chen and Po Chü-i, not knowing, of course, that they were in the presence of one of these poets.[29]

In an essay "On the Dedication of the Stone Tablet of the *Fa-hua Sutra* in Yung-fu Temple," Yüan Chen intimates that the reason for his being called upon to write a dedication piece was due to his exaggerated literary reputation, which he illus-trates with the following evidence. After he was removed from the office of chief minister in 822 and was transferred to Hui-chi in Yüeh-chou, he paid a visit to Hang-chou, where Po Chü-i was prefect at the time. The entire populace poured out to greet him. Impressed by the unprecedented reception given his friend, Po Chü-i asked the spectators the reason for their enthusiasm, and whether it was Yüan Chen's former title of high office that impressed them. The people answered that they came out to see the poet who rivaled Po Chü-i, not because he was the former chief minister.[30]

Similarity in style and matching literary fame linked the

poetry of Yüan Chen and Po Chü-i in the popular mind. Indeed, it must have been difficult to distinguish the poems of one from those of the other. A contemporary of Yüan Chen, Tuan Ch'eng-shih (?–863), in his *Miscellaneous Records of Yu-yang* (*Yu-yang tsa-tsu*), relates that at Chiang-ling he actually saw a common laborer whose body was tattooed with poems by Po Chü-i and illustrated with pictures. It is interesting to note that in relating this episode, Tuan refers to a line from Yüan Chen's "Chrysan-themums," which he mistook to be one of Po Chü-i's poems.[31]

V *The New* Yüeh-fu

Linguistic simplicity and clarity of meaning, which character-ize the poetry of the Yüan-Po school, undoubtedly account for the great popularity of Yüan Chen's poetry. Ironically, those poems that won for him great admiration during his own life-time were not the ones he himself considered to be his most im-portant works. What the poet himself held in highest esteem were those didactic poems containing a social message, satirical or allegorical verse after the Confucian tradition of remonstrat-ing with the ruler or pinpointing the wrongs of the world. These were poems "written with the strongest emotional in-tensity and with blunt, unminced words after the satirical tradition of the *Shih-ching*."[32] Poems implying political criticism and giving voice to social concern were shared only among in-timate friends and patrons who held similar views; they were not widely circulated, because Yüan Chen was "fearful of divulging [them] to the world."[33]

He preferred to write those poems expressing a serious, didactic purpose in the ancient style (*"ku-t'i shih"*), and more specifically, in the *yüeh-fu* style. The *yüeh-fu* genre has had a long and involved historical development. The term originally designated the music bureau, which was instituted by the Wu-ti emperor of Han about 120 B.C. for the purpose of collecting and composing music and songs for various occasions. The *yüeh-fu* repertory covered a wide spectrum of song-poems, ranging from ritual hymns composed at the music bureau to the folk songs collected by bureau officials from the countryside and their later imitations by men of letters. Gradually all the poems thus preserved came to be known to posterity as *yüeh-fu* poetry, regardless of origin, form, or content. Hans R. Frankel, in his comprehensive essay on *yüeh-fu* poetry, provides a succinct definition of this rather confusing term.[34] According to his study, *yüeh-fu* poems comprise seven categories, of which the new *yüeh-fu* of the T'ang dynasty poets is the sixth: "Sixth, some T'ang poets of the eighth and ninth century, such as Yüan Chieh, Po Chü-i, and Yüan Chen, used the term *hsin yüeh-fu* ("new *yüeh-fu* poems") for their poems of social criticism. These were written, like some of the oldest *yüeh-fu* poems, in lines of uneven length; otherwise they were rather different from earlier *yüeh-fu* poetry in their titles, content, and style. They were not set to music."[35]

Most historians tend to attribute the revival of *yüeh-fu* songs to Li Po and Ch'en Tzu-ang, who had adopted the form before Yüan Chen and his circle. However true this may be, there is an essential difference between the *yüeh-fu* poetry of the early T'ang poets and those of Yüan Chen and Po Chü-i: the former had adopted the formal aspects of *yüeh-fu*, such as title, style, the use of uneven lines, and a disregard for tonal euphony; the latter, on the other hand, revived the spirit of the early *yüeh-fu* by consciously adopting a popular folk idiom, thereby bridging the gap that existed between folk songs and the high poetry of the literary class. Moreover, in so doing, they stressed an orthodox, Confucian interpretation of the function of poetry. In a preface to his poems under the category of "*Yüeh-fu* with Ancient Titles," Yüan Chen writes:

From the early *Shih* [*Shih-ching*] up until the oldest *yüeh-fu*, the main thrust in poetry had always been on contemporary affairs through the use of allegory or satire. The purpose was to register a complaint or reaction to a certain event to be transmitted to posterity. Later poets composed to old titles; they harmonized with and reiterated the same themes. Their verses may be short or long, but their intention is never fully exhausted. It seems best to use examples from the past to parallel the events of the present, or to satirize contemporary affairs in the guise of the past. In recent times, fewer and fewer poets have used such methods. Even Ts'ao Chih, Liu Chen, Shen Ch'üan-ch'i, and Pao Chao only rarely took this path. In our own era, only Tu Fu in his "Lamenting Over Ch'en Tao," "Grieving by the River," "The War Chariot," and "Ballad of the Beautiful

Woman" seems to have derived his themes from the *yüeh-fu*, even though not all the titles are identical. During my youth my friends Lo-t'ien [Po Chü-i] and Kung-ch'ui [Li Shen] and I agreed in principle that we would write *yüeh-fu* on contemporary themes with new titles. . . .

Last time at Liang-chou I saw Advanced Scholars Liu Meng and Li Yü. Each of them had written several tens of *yüeh-fu* poems with ancient titles. Among their *yüeh-fu* poems, I found at least a score or two that were impregnated with new meanings. Some of these I have picked out to harmonize with my own compositions. Although these *yüeh-fu* poems bear ancient titles, the content is entirely new. For example, "The Ballad of Leaving Home" [*Ch'u-men hsing*] does not speak of separation, "Offering a Toast" [*Chiang chin chiu*] describes specifically heroic women, etc. Even some of those that are similar to the ancient poems in content, their verbal expressions are entirely new. . . .[36]

This was in 817, when he wrote nineteen *yüeh-fu* with ancient titles; ten of them harmonized with Liu's and nine with Li's. Earlier, in 809, he had written twelve *yüeh-fu* poems with new titles (*hsin-t'i yüeh-fu*) to harmonize with the works of his friend Li Shen, who was the first to write in that form, as Yüan Chen stated in his introductory note to this early group of poems: "My friend Li Kung-ch'ui showed me twenty of his *yüeh-fu* with new titles, which are elegant and worthy of the name of literature. I selected twelve of them that urgently concerned the ills of our times and harmonized them with my own."[37] Yüan Chen then sent his own compositions to Po Chü-i, who then composed fifty of his own in turn, adding thirty-eight new titles of his own.[38]

VI *The Poetic Function*

The *yüeh-fu* with new titles and those with ancient titles both figure in poetic reforms attributable to Yüan Chen. Parallel to the *ku-wen* movement, which focused on prose literature, the poetic reforms of Yüan Chen and his friends did not represent a slavish imitation of the *yüeh-fu* of the past; instead, this was a conscious effort to liberate poetry from the rigid and confining rules of prosody practiced by most of their contemporaries. Unlike the *yüan-ho* style, in which he sought novelty of technique and freshness of diction, experimentation in *yüeh-fu* by Yüan Chen and his friends went beyond innovations in language and style to include the injection of a new seriousness of tone and meaning into *yüeh-fu* verse. Moreover, by adopting the popular meters of the folk lyrics, and by using the common idiom of his own days, Yüan Chen was consciously trying to elevate the folk songs of the populace to the level of respectable literature. This creative effort on Yüan Chen's part has been largely ignored by literary critics, who, overlooking the literary intentions of Yüan Chen and Po Chü-i, dismissed their merits with shallow statements of Yüan's being frivolous and Po's being vulgar.[39]

But the question is not merely one of the use of the common language in verse. It is also one of dominant themes and content. Since Yüan Chen was a statesman by profession and a Confucian by training, it is not surprising that he upheld the traditional Confucian concept regarding the function of poetry: that is, poetry must reveal a serious purpose and not merely serve as an emotional outlet or idle pastime. The same view was shared by his friend Po Chü-i, who maintained that poetry should address itself to rulers, ministers, the people, and contemporary affairs, that it should be didactic, with a social and political content. Poetry with a clear aesthetic appeal could be used to satirize the court, criticize malfunctions in government, and expose the evil deeds of those in power.[40]

Since the literary fame of Po Chü-i has overshadowed that of Yüan Chen for centuries, contemporary critics tend to conclude that the theories of literature Yüan Chen expressed in his writings derived ultimately from Po Chü-i. A close investigation of their own writings, however, points to three other possibilities: (1) that their critical judgments, although similar in most respects, developed independently; (2) that they influenced each other in developing these concepts due to their close personal relationship; and (3) that Po Chü-i derived his ideas from Yüan Chen. There is some reason to believe that the last possibility may be closer to the truth, and I quote from Po Chü-i's letter addressed to Yüan Chen in 816:

... Since you were banished to Chiang-ling [810], I have inflicted upon you, including those that were answers to poems you sent me, a hundred-odd pieces of verse. Whenever you received my poems, you were kind enough to send back to me either an introductory note to them or a letter placed at the beginning of the scroll. and *your subject is always the function of poetry from ancient times until the present.* I, then, make notes myself about the circumstances under which the poems were written and the exact dates on which they were composed. I have always admired your poems; *being now in possession of your ideas about poetry,* I frequently think of putting in rough outline the main principles of this art, together with an account of my own literary intentions, by way of response to your communications.... *It seems to me, however, that what I have to put down will not differ essentially from what you have already stated.*[41]

VII Critical Opinions

Yüan Chen's critical attitudes on the development of Chinese literature are consistent with his belief in the utilitarian function of poetry. The following excerpt from Yüan Chen's introduction to his "Inscription on Tu Fu's tomb,"[42] which represents a thumbnail sketch of the history of Chinese poetry from its earliest beginnings down to his own age, clearly indicates the social orientation of the author's outlook.

In antiquity, during the times of Yao and Shun, kings and ministers responded to one another in song. Later, poets continued to write verse. From the Hsia dynasty until the Chou, a thousand years elapsed. Confucius selected from this millenium three hundred poems which bear didactic and educational values; of the rest, no more was heard.[43] After the creation of the *sao*,[44] expressions of emotional grievances multiplied. However, since *sao* poetry was not too far distant from the days of the *Book of Songs*, it is possible to compare it with portions of the *Book of Songs*. After the Ch'in and Han dynasties abolished the office of collecting poetry, there burst forth upon the world love songs [*yao-yao*], folk songs [*min-o*], hymns [*ko-sung*], satirical prose-poems [*feng-fu*], lyrical measures [*ch'ü-tu*], and humorous rhymes, each following the fashions of the times. During the reign of Wu-ti of Han, the seven character line came into fashion with the *Po-liang* style.[45] Su Wu [fl. second century B. C.] and Li Kuang [d. 125 B. C.], on the other hand, were experts in the five character line.[46]

Although there were great differences in structural forms and rhythms in versification at that time, and the music and tones were varied, and there was an admixture of both the elegant [*ya*] and the seductive [*cheng*],[47] on the whole the language was simple and the intention was far-reaching. Whether they were focusing on certain events or expressing emotions, there was no pure fabrication without substance. After the Chien-an period (196–220), men of letters in the country all suffered from the devastation of war. The works of the Ts'ao family [Ts'ao Ts'ao and his sons Ts'ao P'ei and Ts'ao Chih][48] were frequently composed in the saddle with their lances lying across their laps. That was why their expressions of sadness over life and death followed the ancient tenor. Some of their influence lingered during the Chin dynasty [265–419]. The fundamentals of education were lost during the Sung [420–478] and Ch'i [479–501] regimes [short-lived dynasties in the south during the period of disunity that followed the fall of eastern Chin]; the scholars lapsed into self-indulgence and indolence. They considered as best literature with surface gloss and color and expansive spirit without restraint. Theirs were the writings about their romantic inclinations and prospects of pleasure-seeking; there was not much in meaning and substance, nor vigor in structural form. During the periods of Liang [502–556] and Ch'en [557–588], literature further deteriorated into licentious, erotic, ornamental, and stylistically tricky pieces of art, which was even inferior to that of Sung and Ch'i.

After the founding of T'ang dynasty, public education was widespread. Talents of all kinds and literary styles of all varieties appeared on the scene. Experts in prosody such as Shen and Sung [i.e., Shen Ch'üan-ch'i and Sung Chih-wen] excelled in euphonic balance and parallel structures, thus establishing the fad of regulated verse [*lü shih*]. They have brought great changes in modern versification. . . . However, those who were fond of the ancient style were lost in the contemporary style; those who concentrated on the flowers [the superficial] lacked fruit [the substance]; those who imitated the writers of the Ch'i and the Liang could not maintain the vigor shown in the periods of Wei and the Chin; those who were versed in the *yüeh-fu* were bent to write only the five character lines. To crouch in the regulated form meant to lose one's own natural bone structure; to walk in a leisurely mood was to lose density of texture and intensity of feeling. Then there emerged Tu Tzu-mei [i.e., Tu Fu], who reached clear back to the tradition of the *Shih-ching* and the *Li-sao* of the past and was at home with [the techniques] of Shen Ch'üan-ch'i and Sung Chih-wen. In language he was superior to Su Wu and Li Kuang; in vigor he overpowered Ts'ao Chih [192–232] and Liu Chen [?–217]. Moreover, he soared above the isolated superiority of Yen Yen-nien [384–456] and Hsieh Ling-yün [385–433], and combined the beauty of expression and fluency of style characteristic of Hsü Ling [505–583] and Yü Hsin [513–581]. He had mastered all the poetic aspects from past to present; and he had anticipated all the poetic excellence reached by contemporary poets. . . . No poet of any era, from antiquity until now, is equal to Tu Fu. . . .[49]

Such a superlative eulogy of Tu Fu was not written for conventional reasons but derived from strong convictions, for Yüan Chen found in this model poet all the aesthetic and ethical qualities that he himself aspired to possess. Tu Fu's literary reputation had reached unprecedented heights in the ninth century, so that it is not startling that Yüan Chen held him in great esteem. But what is surprising is that Yüan Chen ventured to compare the literary merits of Tu Fu with those of Li Po, and to cast the latter in an unfavorable light, something unheard of at the time. For it was generally considered that these two celebrated poets of High T'ang, despite their individual differences in lifestyles and aspirations, were equals in their poetic genius. In public opinion, Li Po, the "immortal among poets," represented the culmination of the romantic tendencies in Chinese poetry, whereas Tu Fu, the "sage among poets," had carried the realistic tradition to its highest development; each excelled in his own right. A judgment rating one above the other was thought to reflect the critic's personal bias. At any rate, Yüan Chen was most probably the first person to offer a comparative appraisal of the two, and boldly placed Li Po below Tu Fu in literary merit and creative imagination.

Li Po of Shantung had also acquired great fame by means of his marvelous writing. My contemporaries have joined his name with that of Tu Fu and referred to them collectively as Li-Tu. In my opinion, however, Li Po is really inferior to Tu Fu. He falls short of the heroic vigor and freshness of expression demonstrated in Tu Fu's poems of nature and *yüeh-fu* songs. As for those long poems of a thousand characters, or at least those poems of several hundred characters, which are regulated by the usage of parallelism

from beginning to end and restricted by tonal euphony, Tu Fu alone
could maintain the heroic spirit and linguistic clarity without lapsing
into commonplace. In such areas, Li Po hardly comes near to the
periphery, not to mention the sanctuary of the creative imagination of Tu Fu.[50]

In this passage, the comparison seems to focus on the linguistic
and stylistic differences of the two. Yüan Chen's real bias against
Li Po could have stemmed from the latter's unorthodoxy in poetic
expression as well as in lifestyle. An individualist in rebellion
with the status quo, Li Po's poetry is more arcane and ego-
centered, whereas Tu Fu, on the other hand, is an orthodox
Confucian, who demonstrates the altruistic spirit and social
awareness of the poet engagé. The contrast, according to Arthur
Cooper, is that "between the Dionysian and the Apollonian
aspects of poetry."[51] "It seems a pity," comments Cooper, "that
these two are sometimes categorized, one to be treated sympa-
thetically at the expense of the other, in ways to create a conflict
between them that never existed and that they would not have
understood...."[52]

Yüan Chen's appraisal of Li Po and Tu Fu was shared and
supported by Po Chü-i, who however arrived at a more balanced
evaluation than Yüan Chen had done and was at the same time
more critical of both:

Li's work is talented, even extraordinary. No one else could have
done what he did. But of satire, allegory, double meaning, search
though you may, you will hardly find a trace. Tu Fu was a very
prolific poet and there are over a thousand of his poems that are
quite worth preserving. When it comes to stringing together poems
in the old style or the new and reeling off verse forms and tone
patterns, he does it very skillfully and well; better indeed than Li
Po. But putting them all together, such pieces as "The Recruiting
Officer at Hsin-an," "The Recruiting Officer at Shih-hao," "The Frontier Official at T'ung-kuan," "The Defences at Lu-tzu," and "On the
Detention of the Uigur Troops from Hua-men," or such couplets
as "From the palace gate comes the smell of wine and meat;/ On
the road lie the bones of people who have frozen to death"—it is a
matter of not much more than three or four percent [of his total
corpus].[53]

Such forthright criticism must have infuriated their contemporaries, who were idolators of Li Po and Tu Fu. Han Yü, the great advocate of Confucianism and *ku-wen* prose, who took after Li Po's individualism in his own poetic endeavors, wrote a poem satirizing their views. Although no names are mentioned in the poem, the targets of attack are obviously Yüan Chen and Po Chü-i.

> The poetic splendor of Li and Tu
> Shoots up like flame a myriad feet high.
> Those silly urchins who dare to measure its greatness
> Are like ants and gnats trying to shake a giant tree trunk.[54]

Yüan Chen's theories of literature and critical opinions were unconventional if not entirely unique. In 812, Yüan Chen edited the first collection of his own poems, which were compiled into twenty *chüan*. And he classified them into ten different categories, based on form and content. The following is a summary of his own explanation of the classification system, which he incorporated in a letter to Po Chü-i:[55]

(1) "Satire in ancient air" (*ku-feng*)— poems in the ancient style with specific didactic intentions;

(2) "Satire in *yüeh-fu*" (*yüeh-feng*)—poems in the *yüeh-fu* form but also with didactic intentions;

(3) "*Yüeh-fu* with ancient title" (*yüeh-fu ku-t'i*)— poems in ancient style where the meaning does not go beyond the lyrical expression of emotions;

(4) "New *yüeh-fu*" (*hsin-t'i yüeh-fu*)—the language falls in the *yüeh-fu* category but the theme relates to current affairs and events;

(5) "Five character regulated verse" (*wu-yen lü-shih*)—regulated poems with parallel structure and tonal antithesis in lines of five characters each;

(6) "Seven character regulated verse" (*ch'i-yen ku-shih*)— regulated poems with structural and tonal balance in lines of seven characters each;

(7) "Satire in regulated verse form" (*lü-feng*)—the same prosodic form as (5) and (6) with specific didactic content;

(8) "Elegies" (*tiao-wang shih*)—poems of mourning;

(9) "Ancient style romantic poems" (*ku-t'i yen-shih*);

(10) "Romantic poems in modern style" (*chin-t'i yen-shih*)—same as in (9) in subject matter but written in the modern style.[56]

The above classification was originated by Yüan Chen, and as far as I know, it was perhaps the first time that anyone had attempted a detailed classification of poetry based on form and content at the same time. That Po Chü-i three years later (in 815) also classified his poetic works into fifteen *chüan* under different categories could very well have derived from Yüan Chen. Moreover, Po Chü-i divided his own drafts of imperial rescripts into two groups; the old style, written prior to the reform instituted by Yüan Chen, and the new style written in the "elevated classical style" since the reform. This is another indication that, contrary to general belief, Yüan Chen had a great influence on Po Chü-i. The classification of Po Chü-i's poetry came under four headings: (1) "satirical or remonstrating poems" (*feng-yü shih*), which includes all the new *yüeh-fu* and poems with significant purpose, (2) "poems of leisure" (*hsien-shih shih*), which includes poems of contentment and pleasure of living in retirement; (3) "poems of sad sentiments" (*kan-shang shih*), which includes lyrics inspired by personal experiences of grief; (4) "miscellaneous regulated verse" (*tsa-lü*), which includes all poems written in regulated verse forms.[57] Compared with the classification system Yüan Chen devised for his own poems, this scheme, although much simpler, is less consistently logical in that three of the categories are based on content and one on form, whereas Yüan Chen's system takes both form and content into consideration.

Concern over minute detail was perhaps characteristic with Yüan Chen. In his introduction to his poems grouped under "Yüeh-fu with ancient titles" he lists twenty-four different types of rhythmic literature under the generic term of poetry (*shih*) that are amplifications of the literary genres given in Liu Hsieh's *Wen-hsin tiao-lung*:

The *Shih-ching* [*The Book of Poetry*] was completed during the Chou dynasty; the "Li-sao" ["Encountering Sorrow"] was finished in the state of Ch'u [during the latter part of the Ch'un-ch'iu period, ca. fourth century B. C.]. Since then the rhythmic literature has branched forth into twenty-four categories: *fu* [prose-poetry], *sung* [eulogy], *ming* [mnemonic poetry], *tsan* [laudatory verse], *wen* [expository poetry], *lei* [elegy], *chen* [epigrammic poetry], *shih* [formal poetry], *hsing* [ballad], *yung* [recitative], *yin* [chant], *t'i* [topical verse], *yüan* [plaintive verse], *t'an* [lament], *chang* [explicatory], *p'ien* [sectioned as if by chapters], *ts'ao* [lyrics to be accompanied on the lute], *yen* [prelude], *yao* [folksong], *ou* [rustic rhyme], *ko* [song], *ch'ü* [libretto], *tz'u* [metered lyric], and *tiao* [ditty].[58]

It is obvious that such minute differentiation tends to be redundant and overlapping. As for literary terms of classification, it has been commonly acceptable practice to group them by twos —for example, *yin-yung, tz'u-ch'ü, shih-ko, ko-yao,* and *ko-ch'ü.* In modern usage one usually divides all rhythmic literature into four general categories: *shih, tz'u, ko,* and *fu.* Yüan Chen undoubtedly realized even then that such technical classification as his had more historical value than practical application. He further explains that the eight categories from *ts'ao* to the end of the list are closely related to music, which governs variations of meter, tonal contrast, and euphony. The difference between the *ts'ao* and *yin* depends, for instance, on the different musical instruments that accompany them. On the other hand, the nine categories beginning with *shih* and ending with *p'ien* depend mainly on content. All, however, fall under the generic term of poetry (*shih*): "Later music composers often adopted the themes of the nine categories [beginning with *shih* and ending with *p'ien*] and set them to music according to their verse meters; their composition was not based on music. However, editors of later ages were ignorant of this fact and combined them with the other eight categories, which were music-based, and grouped all the seventeen under the category of *yüeh-fu.*"[59]

The classification of literature by genres had been attempted by many theorists before Yüan Chen's time;[60] but it was rather original of him to make a distinction between poetic genres that were "music-based" and those that were "meter-based." If this particular insight does not qualify him as a literary historian or theorist, it is an indication that scattered in his prose writings there are literary insights that are worth our attention, especially his long letter to Po Chü-i and his "Introduction to the Inscription on Tu Fu's Tombstone."[61] Despite his many contributions to the literature of his own time, he is better known to posterity for his poetry, which we shall turn to next.

CHAPTER 5

The "Poetic Genius"

IN his epitaph for Yüan Chen, dated the twenty-second day of the seventh month of 832, Po Chü-i lamented:

Alas, Wei-chih [the courtesy name of Yüan Chen] lived beyond fifty [the age at which Confucius is said to have known the decree of heaven], so he could not be considered to have been cut down before his time. In politics he had reached the position of chief minister, so he could not be considered undistinguished in official-dom. But he did not fulfill his desire to improve to the utmost the lot of our people, and to manifest the Way [the *Tao*] set by the ancient sages. For this reason it may be said that he died without having fulfilled his goal to his heart's desire. Alas, the Way is broad but the world, of man is narrow; man's ambition is long but man's life is short. Alas, Wei-chih, all is over.[1]

This is certainly no ordinary tomb inscription with stock phrases of conventional praise. Instead of commenting on his friend's achievement in life, Po-Chü-i, who was familiar with his friend's innermost thoughts and aspirations, emphasized Yüan Chen's failure to achieve his own goals, his lack of self-fulfillment. If Yüan Chen had failed as a statesman in carrying out the ideal-istic reforms that he had envisioned in his youth, he did achieve unquestionable success as a poet. In his preface to the same "Tomb Inscription," Po Chü-i describes Yüan Chen's greatness as a man of letters, a master of every literary genre, especially those employing versification. He relates that when Yüan Chen was head of the *Han-lin* Academy, the Mu-tsung emperor had on various occasions requested several hundred of Yüan Chen's poems, which were recited or sung to him by court ladies or musicians. Consequently, Yüan Chen was referred to in the palace as "Yüan, the Genius."[2] Of Yüan Chen's poetry, Po Chü-i

states: "They [Yüan Chen's poems] were copied and circulated
everywhere, including the six palaces and the two capitals, both
at home and abroad, even south to the barbarian states and
far east to foreign countries [Japan and Korea]. Every verse and
every line of his poetry shows intensity and vigor. His language
is as hard and clear as jade and pearls. Yet the intention of his
verse goes far beyond the confines of language and literature.
His goal was to bring peace to the people and order to the
state. . . ."[3]

Yüan Chen himself never underestimated his own poetic
genius. Moreover, he believed in the social influence of his
poetry. It was not sheer bragging but a recognition of his own
merit as poet when he wrote:

> My ideas may not be prolific, but my poetry is genuine
> And its meter suitable for strings.
> All three capitals hold my verse in esteem,
> In time the world will see its beauty.

Since the poem was addressed to Po Chü-i, the lines that follow
can be taken to include his friend's poetry as well as his own
when he says:

> Musicians sing our poems at banquets;
> School boys recite them in the street.
>
> . . . .
>
> The poetry of the Wei dynasty may look dull by comparison,
> With the prestige of the Ts'aos we dare to compete.
> Though our verse might draw laughter from true genius,
> I fear it has become a craze among neophytes.[4]

Yüan Chen's intention of using poetry to express his socio-
political ideas is succinctly stated in his "Letter to Lo-t'ien Concerning Poetry," which is a combination of an *ars poetica* and
an *autobiographia literaria*. In this letter he first relates his
early interest and training in poetry: "I learned how to compose in the *shih* and *fu* forms when I was eight years old. My
elders frequently marveled at my aptitude in learning. By the
time I was fourteen I could detect any flaw of euphony in

versification. . . ."[5] Further on, he describes in great detail the social evils and political corruption incurred by the military governors he had witnessed in the provinces (such as Feng-hsiang in Shensi), and how these governors ignored imperial orders and exploited the masses in the name of tribute, or how corrupt officials and their underlings robbed the populace of their livelihood. Then he continues:

Yet great ministers at court, for fear of reprisal or to protect their own interests, held their peace. The few who dared remonstrate were usually demoted or dispatched to remote regions or even imprisonment. . . . I was very young and not yet immune to what I had heard or seen. When I began to differentiate, through reading the classics, between good government and corrupt government, my heart trembled and my body shook as if I could not continue living. I had harbored the wish to expose and make known what I had experienced for a long time. . . .[6]

The first poetic endeavor of Yüan Chen resulted in poems in the manner of Ch'en Tzu-ang's twenty poems entitled *Kan-yü shih* (Poems of Personal Reactions to Happenings). The budding poet showed his own series of twenty poems (no longer extant) entitled "To Master Szu-hsüan" (*Chi Szu-hsüan-tzu shih*) to his maternal grandfather, Cheng Chi, then mayor of the capital. Cheng was so impressed with the poems that he turned to his friend Wang Piao, assistant director of the palace library, and remarked, "If this youngster lives beyond fifty without losing such noble sentiments, it would be something for us to look forward to. Unfortunately, our generation will not be here to witness his achievement."[7]

It is impossible to determine whether or not Yüan Chen lived up to his grandfather's expectations, but there is no denying his achievement as a poet. Even those who viewed his verse with disdain could not but acknowledge the impact of Yüan Chen's poetry on his contemporaries. Since the response to poetry varies from person to person and from age to age, it is difficult to judge the true quality of a poet by his popularity or lack of it. There is no doubt, however, that the poetry of Yüan Chen and Po Chü-i was very popular during their own lifetimes, especially during the *yüan-ho* and *ch'ang-ch'ing* periods, which also produced a number of other prominent poets, such as Han Yü, Meng Chiao, Li Ho, and Liu Yü-hsi. A late T'ang poet, Tu Mu, an outspoken critic of Yüan Chen and Po Chü-i, put his own adverse criticism of their poetry in the mouth of a third party, Li K'an, a little known scholar for whom Tu Mu wrote an epitaph. In his introduction to Li K'an's tomb inscription, Tu Mu quoted Li K'an as saying:

The richness or poverty of a nation's culture depends largely on poetry, which affects it with the swiftness of the wind. I grieve over the fact that since the *yüan-ho* reign the poetry of Yüan Chen and Po Chü-i, which is both trivial and extravagant, and lacking in restraint, has prevailed. With the exception of those who were steadfast, serious scholars with innate moral principles, everyone has been exposed to their destructive influences. Their poems have been widely circulated among the common people; they were even copied on walls and screens and were taught by word of mouth from father to son, mother to daughter. Their lascivious and wanton expressions are like the winter cold and summer heat that penetrate one's flesh and bones; once subjugated to their influences it becomes irremediable.[8]

Although the above comment roundly condemns the poetry of Yüan Chen and Po Chü-i, it nevertheless attests eloquently to their popularity as leading poets of the day. Since Po Chü-i's poetry has been dealt with extensively elsewhere,[9] I shall concentrate in the following pages on Yüan Chen's poems only. No critical appraisal of Yüan Chen's poetry can be undertaken without a close reading of his poems, for the proof of the pudding is in the tasting. Ideally, however, all poetry should be read in the original, especially Chinese poetry, since such features as rhyme and rhythm, which are lost in translation, constitute key elements in the physical structure of a poem. Yet, in order to introduce Yüan Chen's poetry to the reader who may not know Chinese, we must resort to translation, which, at best, can capture only the spirit that is inherent in the original. The poems represented here are arranged according to subject matter, not by verse form, because in translation it is almost impossible to reproduce accurately the linguistic and prosodic features of the original. It is hoped that one may obtain a clearer image of Yüan Chen the man and the poet through the reading of his poems than the vague impressions derived from literary gossip and hearsay reports.

I *Poems of Social and Political Concern*

A. "Lien-ch'ang Palace"

A pragmatic scholar imbued with the Confucian tradition, Yüan Chen firmly believed that poetry could be used as a means to effect social and political changes. Consequently, an ideal poet must be primarily didactic. Understandably, he put his beliefs into practice, although he occasionally wrote verse of a personal nature, such as expressions of personal joy or sorrow; or as a literary pastime; or as entertainment or communication with friends. However, the poems that he treasured most in his own works as well as in the works of others were those containing a social message. For to him the message constitutes the soul and breath of poetry, while the language, rhythm, and structure are formal aspects only. In other words, an ideal poem must possess edifying sentiments alongside its pleasurable attributes in verbal expression.

One of the most exemplary of Yüan Chen's political poems is "Lien-ch'ang Palace" (*Lien-ch'ang kung tz'u*), a new *yüeh-fu* in ninety lines (with seven characters to each line). The exact date of its composition is unknown. According to internal evidence, it could not have been written prior to the spring of 815, nor later than the year 818, because it describes late spring in its opening lines and makes reference to the rebellion at Huai-hsi, which did not break out until 815, and to the fact that its rebel leader, Wu Yüan-chi (783–817), had not yet been captured.[10]

"Lien-ch'ang Palace" is decidedly a political poem, voicing freely Yüan Chen's own antimilitary attitudes and questioning the government's responsibility in regard to the causes of war and peace. The criticism, however, is typically veiled, for the poem is set in the historical past. In addition, it ends with a note of hopeful expectation for the future, thereby revealing the essentially optimistic and Confucian turn of mind of the poet.

Lien-ch'ang Palace was built in 658, approximately seventy-six *li* west of the eastern capital, Lo-yang. It was one of several temporary palaces on the route between the two capitals of Lo-yang and Ch'ang-an that were used for the comfort and convenience of the emperors when they made excursions from one capital to another. In this long narrative poem Lien-ch'ang Palace is singled out to serve as a focus of action and a point of departure. The poet-observer appears to be passing in front of Lien-ch'ang Palace on a late spring day, when he meets an old peasant who is a native to the area, a survivor of the *t'ien-pao* era more than half a century before. An eyewitness to the vicissitudes of time, the peasant-narrator provides firsthand information on what took place at the palace, which functions as a symbol of the dynasty itself, before and after the An Lu-shan Rebellion. In the poem, Yüan Chen is a passive listener-recorder who sets the stage for the peasant to begin his story with a brief description of the neglected palace grounds, and only once does he intrude before the conclusion of the poem.

As a work of art, "Lien-ch'ang Palace" is possibly superior to Po Chü-i's famous "Song of the Everlasting Sorrow" (*Ch'ang-hen ko*) in the complexity of its structure and in its rich texture of social and political implications.[12] Po's poem, for instance, centers on the tragic story of the Hsüan-tsung emperor and his favorite consort, Yang Kuei-fei.[13] If it contains any social message at all, it is overshadowed by the romantic treatment of the love theme between the tragic pair and diffused by the superimposed supernatural tale of Yang Kuei-fei's life after death. In "Lien-ch'ang Palace," on the other hand, the royal couple is introduced to serve an artistic purpose only: to achieve a temporal contrast between the glorious past of the *t'ien-pao* period and the deplorable state of affairs of the postrebellion era. In addition, whether it was intended or not, this poem is believed to have played a significant role in Yüan Chen's own political career. It had been rumored that his ascendancy to power during the *ch'ang-ch'ing* period was due largely to this poem.

According to one story, after the Mu-tsung emperor came to the throne, a eunuch, Ts'ui T'an-chün, who had become acquainted with and had great admiration for Yüan Chen during the latter's exile in the provinces, brought the poet's works to the attention of the new emperor, who before he came to the throne had already been familiar with Yüan Chen's poetry. The peace policy expressed in "Lien-ch'ang Palace" especially pleased the monarch, and he enquired immediately as to the poet's whereabouts. After a quick succession of promotions Yüan Chen was installed in the *Han-lin* Academy, there to be in charge of the drafting of imperial rescripts. Within a year, he was further promoted to the position of chief minister.[14] Whether or not the poem was responsible for Yüan Chen's political success during the *ch'ang-ch'ing* era, it is a poem worth reading for its rich imagery and narrative techniques.

[Poem 1]

Lien Ch'ang Palace[15]

Lien-ch'ang Palace is overgrown with bamboo,
Long years untended, it has turned into a thicket;
The double-flowering peach trees, towering above the walls,
Shed red showers when the wind stirs.

By the palace gate an old man with tears told me: 5
"Once in my youth I was there to bring food to the palace.
The Grand Emperor was in Wang-hsien Hall,
T'ai-chen leaned against the railing by his side.
Above the hall and in front, whirled jade and pearls,
Sparkling, reflecting heaven and earth.   10
I left as if in a dream, with my senses gone.
How could I relate in full these palace affairs?

"The Feast of Cold Food had just come,
      a hundred and six days after winter solstice,
No chimney smoke rose from rooftops
      and palace trees were turning green.
At midnight when the moon was high   15
      string music was heard upstairs—
Master Ho's *p'i-p'a* set the stage for chamber music.

"Then Eunuch Kao called out the order to find Nien-nu,
Who was elsewhere entertaining her guests in private.
Soon she was found and urged to hurry;
By special edict, the streets were lit with candles.   20
A scene of spring loveliness, she lay amid red silk;
Tidying her cloudlike hair, she hurriedly dressed.

"When she sang her voice soared to the ninth heaven,
Followed by the treble of Prince Pin's flute.
The twanging music of Liang-chou filled the palace,   25
The deeper tunes of Kuchah followed along.
Outside the palace wall, holding his flute,
Li Mu stole several new melodies he overheard.

"At dawn the imperial entourage departed from Lien-ch'ang,
And thousands of people danced in joy along the road;   30
Processions of officials avoided the path of Princes Ch'i
         and Hsüeh;
In their carriages, the Yang sisters raced with the wind.

"In the tenth month of the following year, the Eastern
         Capital fell:
The imperial road, still intact, the rebels now trod.
Pressed for provisions, no one dared to hide.   35
Silently the people shed secret tears.

"Six or seven years after both capitals were restored,
I came back to search for my homesite near this palace—
The village was razed by fire, only dried wells remained;
The palace gate was shut: trees and gardens were still there.   40

"Since that time six emperors have ascended the throne,
But Lien-ch'ang Palace remains long unvisited.
Young travelers coming here, talked about Ch'ang-an:
They said Hsüan-wu Tower was now completed, but Hua-o
         abandoned.

"Last year an order came to cut down the palace bamboo,   45
By chance I found the gate open and stepped in:
Thorns and brambles thickly clogged the imperial pond,
Proud foxes and doltish hares capered about among the trees;
The dance pavilion had collapsed, its foundation still there;
The ornamented windows were dim, but the screens still green;   50
Dust covered the old filigree on painted walls;
Crows had pecked the wind chimes, scattering pearls and jade.

"The Grand Emperor enjoyed terraced flowers,
His royal couch still lay aslant above the garden steps.
Snakes emerged from swallows' nests and coiled on beams;   55
Mushrooms grew out of the altar in the central hall.

Adjoining the royal bedchamber was Tuan-cheng Tower
Where T'ai-chen once washed and combed her hair.
In the early dawn the curtains which cast dark shadows—
Even now, are hung by coral hooks, upside down.   60

"Pointing out these things to others, I could not but grieve,
My tears continued to fall long after I left the palace.
Since then the palace gate has been closed once more,
Night after night foxes enter the gate and towers."

Hearing his words, I ached in my heart and bones: 65
Who brings peace to the empire? Who brings war?
"What difference is there," said the old man,
     "to a peasant like me?
I only tell of what my ears have heard and my eyes have seen.

"When Yao Ch'ung and Sung Ching were ministers
Their counsel to the emperor was firm and earnest.   70
The *yin* and *yang* were in accord, the harvest was full;
Harmony prevailed and peace reigned over the land,
High officials were upright, local magistrates just.
For they were all chosen by the ministers.

"The *k'ai-yüan* period closed with the death of Yao and Sung,   75
Gradually, the imperial consort had her way at court.
Into the palace, she brought An Lu-shan as her 'adopted son';
The front of Madame Kuo's palace was busier than a marketplace.

"I have forgotten the names of those powerful ministers
But vaguely remember they were Yang and Li   80
Who caused turmoil in government that shook the four seas—
For fifty years the nation has groaned from its wounds.

"Our present emperor is wise and the ministers have foresight,
No sooner came the imperial order than Wu and Shu surrendered;
Now government troops have captured Huai-hsi from the rebels;   85
When those rebels are caught the world will be at peace.
For years we have tilled the wasteland before the palace,
Now I won't send my sons and theirs to do the plowing."
I am deeply moved by the old man's story;
Let's direct our efforts to put an end to all wars.   90

                              (*YSCCC* 24/297–300)

B. Other Poems of Social Concern

Yüan Chen's antiwar attitudes, voiced by the old peasant in "Lien-ch'ang Palace," are expressed in different terms in the poem "Husbands Drafted." It tells of the grief of wives whose husbands are sent off to war. Written in the *yüeh-fu* form with an ancient title, it relates an historical incident of the state of Chao during the period of the warring states (403-221 B.C.), when war was waged almost continuously between the feudal lords and their followers. The story centers upon Chao Kua (fl. third century B.C.), who was the son of Chao She, a famous general of the state of Chao. From his early youth, Chao Kua's sole interest in life was warfare, to the great dismay of his father, who predicted that Kua would bring about the downfall of the state of Chao. When war broke out with Ch'in, the prince of Chao appointed Chao Kua to be the commanding general, succeeding his deceased father, and despite his mother's protests and warning. Chao Kua was defeated and his army of 450,000 men completely annihilated. Although the events related in the poem belonged to a remote past, the fear and grief of the women must have seemed as real to Yüan Chen's time as it still does today.

[Poem 2]

Husbands Drafted[16]

Four hundred fifty thousand men of the state of Chao
All became ghosts in a common grave.
The Chao prince ignored the warning of the mother of Chao Kua.
Drafted new men and drove them to their doom.
The draftees' morale was low,   5
With no effort the Ch'in army crushed Chao;

Despite Kua's ability to withstand Pai Ch'i,
The latter's tactics outwitted Kua's fixed purpose.
And Chao Kua was hampered and pulled down
By the dead in the ditches, and their widows in camp.   10

Draped in white garments and with hemp in their hair
They lamented wildly like the honking of wild geese.
Those who saw their husbands off cried equally loud,
As if mourning their death rather than parting in life.

Their husbands are drafted! 15
Draftees need not go so far as the Great Wall;
Once they leave the city gate,
There is no difference between life and death.

(*YSCCC* 23/286–87)

[Poem 3]

The Farmer

The water buffalo bellows,
The earth crackles,
Clods of dried earth fall from the buffalo's hoofs.

He plows the field to fill the public granary:
For sixty years soldiers roamed everywhere, 5
Month after month the supply cargoes rolled.

One day the government troops reached the frontier,
They slaughtered his buffalo and confiscated his cart;
He returned home with only two buffalo horns.

Then he worked with a spade forged from a plowshare; 10
Sister threshing, wife toting, off he goes to pay taxes again;
Not enough, then he is forced to sell his house.

I pray for an early victory of the state.
The farmer may die, he may still have an heir— 15
And the buffalo, its calf,
But let there be no shortage of military supplies.

(*YSCCC* 23/287–88)

"The Farmer" is one of Yüan Chen's most frequently anthologized poems, partly because of its brevity and simplicity, partly
because of its sense of pathos. That governmental exactions in
times of war can jeopardize the very existence of the noncom-
batant just as it does that of the soldier is exemplified in the experience of the poor farmer, who is as much a victim of war
as those sacrificing their lives on the front line. An interesting
ambiguity characteristic of Yüan Chen's satirical style is to be
found in the final stanza, where one cannot be sure whether
the poet is speaking with tongue in cheek, or whether ironically
the ignorant farmer is declaring his loyalty to the government

despite his personal loss. In either case, the meaning of the poem is quite clear: the mindless destruction of human life and society is the price of war.

[Poem 4]
Song of Building the Great Wall
(in five stanzas)

Year after year the men at the frontier
Serve as soldiers on the front line.
After Mao Tun of the Huns rose to power,
We built the Great Wall to keep the barbarians out.

We built the wall with all the strength we possess: 5
The wall must be high enough to fend off those bandits;
But the bandits have many ways to approach;
Even the wall cannot block them.

From mouth to mouth, told by young to old:
"Don't ask if the wall is solid. 10
When P'ing-ch'eng was encircled by the Huns
The emperor of Han could escape only by knocking the wall down.

"Now the Huns have asked for peace
And, in retreat, their troops ride by.
Half doubting, half believing their words 15
We keep building the wall as high as cliffs."

How dare I complain about building the Great Wall?
But I would that you give heed to one laborer's advice:
"First build an office of foreign diplomacy,
Then see if the Huns will stay out of the Great Wall." 20

(*YSCCC* 23/294)

To Yüan Chen, as indeed to many of his friends in the same political camp, the military solution is not a real solution to social problems. Strong military forces may quell insubordination and rebellion temporarily, if at all, but they can not root out the causes of war and rebellion. Not only does Yüan Chen advocate peaceful means and benevolent rule in dealing with domestic problems, but regarding the surrounding barbarian tribes, such as the Huns, he feels that the Great Wall itself is no real deterrent to invasion from the north. Peaceful coexistence can be reached, not through stronger national defense, but through diplomacy.

P'ing-ch'eng is a city east of modern Ta-t'ung county in Shensi. When Kao-tzu of Han (r. 206–194 B.C.) fought against the Huns, he and his troops in P'ing-ch'eng were encircled by the enemy. On the seventh day, Kao-tzu ordered the soldiers to knock down the city wall in order to break out of the encirclement. P'ing-ch'eng later became the capital of the Toba Wei, which ruled most of North China (386–534).

Constant warfare meant the continuous conscription of soldiers, hard labor for all, exorbitant taxation, and a dearth of agricultural products. Government exactions of one kind and another imposed heavy burdens on the people, burdens made even heavier by official greed and corruption. The government paid fifty pieces of silk in trade for a Uigur horse. When this trade increased, either because of higher demands for foreign horses by government officials or for silk by foreign countries, the quotas for silk production had to be doubled or tripled. As a consequence, the weaving women were forced to enslave themselves to the loom for longer hours. Yüan Chen's sympathy is clearly with this oppressed class, as is seen in the following poem:

[Poem 5]

Song of the Weaving Woman[17]
(Translated by Wu-chi Liu)

Busy is the life of the weaving woman!
Silkworms are about to grow old after their third sleep,
And soon the silkworm goddess will start to make silk;
Early too comes this year's levy of the silk tax.

This early tax is not the evil doing of the officials—   5
The government has been waging wars since last year:
Soldiers in bitter fighting bandage their sword wounds;
The great general, his merits high, changes his gauze curtain.

She'd continue her effort to reel threads and weave silk,
But the tangled skeins on the loom give her trouble.   10

In the house to the east, a white-haired man has two daughters;
He wouldn't marry them off because they're skilled in embroidery.
Amid the floating gossamers on the eaves,
A spider nimbly plies back and forth.
Admirable are the insects that understand heaven's way;   15
They know how to spin a gossamer web in the void.

                                                    (*YSCCC* 23/287)

The poet's compassion for the weaving women whose father
would not allow them to marry and be fulfilled according to
the way of nature (the *yin-yang* principle decreed by heaven)
is extended to another category of women. Palace women enjoy
a more leisurely life than poor weaving maids. But their fate is
equally pitiable, perhaps even worse than that of the weaving
women, for they are snatched from their homes, from their husbands or fathers, and placed in the palace against their will.
Picked by imperial envoys for their beauty, many remained in
the palace, doomed to a living death, never to be married or
to have a family of their own. The "white-haired" palace maid
was but one of thousands of such women who led useless,
frustrated lives. The poem is a remonstration in the name of
the past against the current practice of the Hsien-tsung emperor,
whose harem was heavily populated. In the last stanza, Yüan
Chen reiterates some concrete suggestions that he had developed
in his famous "Ten Point Proposal" to the emperor in 806, stating
that in order to keep in balance the *yin* and *yang* elements at
court, the number of palace women should be reduced by
allowing some to leave the palace and marry.

[Poem 6]
                The White-haired Lady at Shang-yang Palace[18]

The imperial envoy, the "beauty scout" of the *t'ien-pao* era,
Ravished the flowers and hounded the fowls, lecherous in
        his spring thoughts.
With the royal order to select beauties for the palace,
He climbed to high places in a state of drunkenness.
Brazenly he would enter reputable residences unannounced,   5
So the ladies could not find time to hide themselves.
Young wives were torn away from their husbands as if by death;
Young daughters called out for their fathers, weeping bloody tears.

Perhaps only one out of ten maidens thus snatched away
Was delivered to the Forbidden City to be palace maids.   10

The imperial steed sped south, the barbarian horses pressed on;
Three thousand palace maidens were abandoned.
The palace was closed, never to open again.
Now the flower garden of Shang-yang Palace is covered with
    green moss;
Moss grows where flowers and green lawns were.   15

"On moonlit nights I listen to the soul of the Lo River;
By the autumn pond I smell lotus hidden in the breeze.
Day in and day out I watch the Ti-hsiang Gate,
But never have I seen what transpired outside the gate.
In recent years a few more maidens arrived—   20
Brought in from the southern palace of Hsing-ch'ing."

Her song grieved me deep in my bones,
Thinking on the wrongs suffered by her lot reduced me to tears.
Who would care for such humble creatures as palace maids?
Princes and royal heirs are time-honored,   25
But they have been imprisoned for forty years,
Since the seven mansions and six palaces were all shut down.

But scions of Sui-yang were all enfeoffed,
But Su-tsung's brothers held no offices.
The princes have no consorts, the princesses no mates;   30
With *yang* waning, the *yin* overflowing, mishaps mount.
Why not eliminate obstacles and follow the law of nature:
Let maidens take husbands and allow the male to work.

                    (*YSCCC* 24/303)

[Poem 7]

Song of the Pearl Fishers

    Fathomless are the waves;
        Pearls lie deep in the sea.
    In vain the pearl fishers risk their lives:
    Ten thousand are doomed,
        Yet perhaps one may find pearls.   5
    Where is he who measured out pearls
        In exchange for servant girls?

Year after year men have gone after pearls
    And pearls have managed to elude them.
This year pearls are gathered by the god of the sea;   10
    Gathered by him, all the pearls are gone;
Empty is the sea, devoid of bright pearls.

The pearls belong to the sea,
    And the sea to the sea god;
Now the sea god himself will gather the pearls,   15
    What can there be left for man?
                    (*YSCCC* 23/285)

It had been a traditional custom for local officials of the southern and eastern coastal regions to offer annual tributes of pearls to the throne. Yüan Chen found the quota for local tribute pearls unreasonable, especially in view of the risks taken by the pearl fishers, many of whom indeed lost their lives in their work. The poem is a plea for the discontinuance of such practices, which provided immense profits for intermediaries in charge of collection and transportation. Few, however, were concerned about the dangers to the poor people involved, those who were employed as pearl fishers.

Greed for profit was not confined to those in official capacities who exacted sweat and blood from the poor. The merchant class, which derived profit from exploitation rather than from its own productive efforts, is described by Yüan Chen as contributing to governmental corruption. "The Pleasure of Being a Merchant" is not so much a satire on the merchant or small businessman from a typical Confucian antimercantile point of view as it is a satire on the power of money, criminally acquired, to generate power and control over government officials who are supposedly there to prevent crime and injustice.

[Poem 8]
The Pleasure of Being a Merchant

The merchant has no permanent address;
Where there is profit, there he goes.

First he goes out to look for partners,
Then he bids farewell to his father and elder brother.

And here are their parting instructions: 5
"Look only for profit; don't look for fame.
For fame you need caution in your actions;
For profit there is no limit to what you can do.
Partners are burdensome to one another;
Sell falsehood and don't sell truth.   10
Pay the duties with fake figures
So your gain seems less than your loss."
Equipped with their wisdom he sets forth,
Swearing never to stray from such course.

Having learned the jargon of the peddler's trade,   15
He has no feelings for fellowship.
Using brass he forged into gold bracelets,
With rice powder he blew into jade necklaces,
He returns to his native village to sell his wares,
Making them sound like gold and precious stone.   20
Village wenches and peasant women
Dare not haggle or dispute prices with him,
So for the capital of a hundred cash
He takes a profit of ten times more.
His color is improved, his cheeks glow,   25
Sweet and savory are his food and drink.
Interests and capital all multiplied.
Day by day his business increases.

In search of pearls he sails on the vast sea;
To collect gems he goes to Ching-chou and Heng-yang.   30
From the north he buys Tangut steeds,
From the west he purchases the parrots of Tibet.
There is fire-proofed cloth from the tropics,
And satin brocade from Szechwan,
Slave girls from Yüeh with skin silky like lard,   35
And Tartar boys with bright eyes and clear brows.
He does not grudge food or lodging,
Nor does he reckon the distance.
Having traveled everywhere under heaven
He finally arrives at Ch'ang-an.   40

The eastern and western markets of the city
Welcome him in succession.
They welcome him and they offer him advice:
Great wealth must have political backing.

The merchant is shrewd at heart;   45
He is quick to heed the alert.
He first seeks out the ten intendants;
Then he begs to see the ministers.
The palaces of princes and dukes
Are supplied with rare and marvelous things.   50

Only then does he sit back feeling secure,
And vying for wealth with the lords.
The city police become sated with his meat and drink,
The county sheriffs are offered houses for free,
So that they not only hang on his words   55
But run to carry out his wishes.
His elder son is in the lumber business now,
And expert on beams and pillars;
His younger son trades in salt
And never has to pay taxes to the state.   60

When one person succumbs to the profits of the market
It is like having a whale blocking the sea:
No one dares to taunt it with hooks or spikes
For fear of its powerful teeth.
O the pleasure of being a merchant!   65
I bet you enjoy a pleasurable life.
Now you also have two merchant sons,
But when will there ever be monetary equity?
                                (*YSCCC* 23/294–95)

C.   Allegories and Animal Fables

Although Yüan Chen, more often than not, is straightforward
in his comments on general issues of social injustice as illustrated
by the poetry cited above, he occasionally resorts to the use of
animals and plants to describe certain people or types of people
whom he dares not attack openly. "The Big-Billed Crows" is a
political allegory where the master possibly stands for the
emperor, the crane and the eagle represent loyal and able
ministers, while the big-billed crows may be either wicked
eunuchs or treacherous ministers.[20]

[Poem 9]

The Big-Billed Crows[21]

Crows are of two sorts:
The white-beaked are called benign birds;

They seek food to feed the mother bird,
That is how they got this name.
They drink and pick frugally,   5
Their cawing is gentle.
They build a hundred nests on the same tree,
Living together with no suspicion.
When they find food they first offer it to the mother birds,
Willing to go hungry themselves.   10
Because they seem to understand human relationships,
They are bullied by other fowl.

The other type of crow is the big-billed:
A bird of prey, greedy and stupid,
They have the strength of the hawk,   15
Their claws are sharp like awls.
Their cawing is monstrous
As if communicating with the evil spirit;
Bathed in the splendor of the sun
There seems no limit to their lifespan.   20
They fly about the houses of the rich
Or perch on a branch in front of their doors.
The witch says that whenever this crow arrives
The family's wealth will daily increase.

The master of the house being deceived   25
Tirelessly tries to lure the crow.
When he sees it flying about
He tells himself his fortune will grow.
Neither the white crane in front of the gate
Nor the variegated falcon on the stand   30
Can vie for the master's attention with the crow,
Which is treated as if it were a sacred tortoise.
The whole family agrees with him
And put aside their slingshots.
Frequently by the edge of the clear pool   35
The crow is seen leading the cranes.
Fed with choice morsels of meat and grain
Its plumage gains a glossy sheen.

Freely the crow comes and goes and does what it pleases;
Endless are its cruel and rapacious ways: 40
It robs others' nests of fledglings and eggs;
And pecks the wounds of stabled horses.

Drained and exhausted are nature's resources,
But how is the phoenix to know of it?

.   .   .   .

(YSCCC 1/9)

The following poem, "An Ode to Cloud-Gazing Dapple," on
the other hand, is a narrative based on certain historical facts,
but fictionalized and allegorized so that the horse represents
loyal officials who are forgotten after their missions have been
accomplished. The meaning of the poem is unmistakeable. One
can hardly miss the twinge of self-pity when the poet grieves
over the fate of the displaced horse.

[Poem 10]

An Ode to Cloud-Gazing Dapple[22]
(With an Introduction)

When the Te-tsung emperor graced Szechwan, eight horses were
selected for imperial use. Seven of them died en route; Cloud-Gazing
Dapple alone accomplished his mission without fail. Later, the horse
died of old age in the imperial stables. I wrote this poem to commemorate this extraordinary steed.

Remember when Te-tsung traveled to Szechwan—
Eight horses entered the valley and seven were spent:
Their flesh torn, with tendons exposed, their hooves worn,
One by one, seven of the eight steeds expired.
The Son of Heaven was covered with mud and heaven wept;   5
The wet road along the precipitous slopes was dangerously slippery.
The lofty Pai-ts'ao was forbidding as the Yellow Springs;
Before the encirclement of Chu Tzu was withdrawn,
The rebel troops of Huai Kuang were pressing near.   10
The court ladies looked at each other and wept against the trees;
Royal attendants stood there silently staring into the skies.

Hesitant, the groom brought forth Cloud-Gazing Dapple,
Looking haggard because he was abused by other horses.
But he stepped forward with meaningful neighs,   15
With ears pricked up; he stood tall, though his joints looked odd.
The emperor was about to dismiss him and then changed his mind.
For the horse had a fine frame, jagged teeth, and well-joined ribs;
His head was square, his stride as wide as three hillocks,
His tail straight and strong like a tree trunk.   20

"This horse is no good, even if it's strong:
It bites, and tears, and resists the bridle;
It leaps and rears and refuses to be saddled," cried the grooms.
Despondent, they moaned and complained to heaven,
But heaven sent no signs the emperor could understand.   25
Lowering its body, the horse received the white jade saddle;
And opening its mouth it submitted to the bit of purple gold.
Only then did the emperor dare to mount the dapple,
Who, like a loyal minister, had been longing for this moment.
Like a dragon he soared, startling the fish and turtles;   30
The mules and donkeys cringed at the sight of the thoroughbred.
The Seven Sages lost their way, perilous their fate;
The Five Strong were spent, the road was still too narrow.
On Mount Camel were heaps of axe blades;
Below the ranges of Ch'in, the rocks were formed like awls.   35
Chen-fu was five to six hundred *li* away,
And there were yet eighty-four winding turns to the Ch'ing-shan post;
But the dapple sped on like a flash of lightning
Rushing through the floating clouds, leaving no trace.
At last the ground leveled and the danger passed: 40
The emperor could ride in his yellow royal coach
Attended by eighty-one carriages and twelve banners.
Ch'i Ying led the dapple to head the procession;
Yen Chen, coming to welcome his sire, embraced the dapple's legs.
Along the road, the gray survivors of the *t'ien-pao* reign   45
Greeted the dapple with reverence and tears.
"What a pity that Emperor Hsüan-tsung had no horse like this,
Then he would not have come on a mule."
The heroic and fearless General Li
Restored the capital, killed the rebels   50
And rid the nation of all ravening wolves.
After the revolution of heaven and earth,
The sun was once more restored to the center of the cosmos,
And the Son of Heaven sat again in the Illustrious Palace.
The court, free from trouble, had forgotten the wars;   55
The days were engaged in hunting expeditions
And the evenings in polo games and carousing.
All the imperial horses were tested for drawing chariots;
The emperor himself examined them in Hsüan-hui Hall.
The groom again brought forth Cloud-Gazing Dapple,   60
But the beast was deemed unfit, being too spirited
And his strides too wide, his mane too sparse, his head held too high;

His elbows were torn, and he could hardly turn his neck.
Everyone detested him for not easily turning around,
So the flying dragon was led away with his fodder reduced.   65
The silver saddle and embroidered trappings were no longer his;
In vain he spent his last days in the imperial stable.
There was a saying at that time:
"Don't depend on past merit to ride on the crest."
To climb the mountains one needs Cloud-Gazing Dapple;   70
On level ground, one prefers the red Arabian.
In the spring of Ch'ang-an when flowers are touching the grass
Trotting under the fruit trees is the sorrel most elegant.
Thousands of officials bask in the warmth of the court
But General Li was left in the cold;   75
Hundreds of horses grew fierce but the Dapple grew old.
O Cloud-Gazing Dapple, yours is a rare breed in any age.
Once the great King Hsiang of Ch'u rode your ancestor,
Whose heroism matched that of his master, the Hegemon;
You encountered a sage in your lifetime,   80
And carried him to Szechwan and returned him to Ch'in.
Retreat following success is the way of heaven:
Why tramp in the red dust until death?
Cloud-Gazing Dapple, there is time to serve or not to serve.
Do not grieve!   85

(*YSCCC* 24/300–302)

On the surface, "Spring Cicada" may be taken simply as a poem of nature. Yet one can easily detect the political message it conveys, especially in the last stanza, where the poet expresses the desire that heaven purge the evil, unhealthy climate from his area of exile, but, by extension, from the imperial court, which was infested with treacherous eunuchs.

[Poem 11]

Spring Cicada

Since I returned from the east
I have been annoyed by the daily cooing of spring doves.
I wrote verse to plead with Creation
Not to breed cicadas in spring.

Now that I am on the road to Shang-shan,   5
Where the weather along the mountain path is uneven;

Where spring and autumn are alike,
The clamor of hundreds of birds and insects
Upsets the rhythm of wind passing through the pines.
Swarms of cicadas babble like boiling broth;   10
But the phoenix soars toward the sun,
Unwilling to look upon such base creatures.

How I wish that the rain would come
And pour down from heaven like a toppling sea
To purge all the unseasonal air,   15
So there will be fair weather ahead, and clear skies.
                                              (*YSCCC* 1/3)

Not only animals, but plants also are used allegorically to convey social or political meaning. The dodder plant, generally
known as a love vine, is used in the following poem to symbolize
the ineffectual officials who cling to one political faction or
another for their existence. At the same time, the poem may
be taken simply as a philosophical axiom that the poet wishes
to impart to others.

[Poem 12]

The Dodder Plant[23]

In life don't be a clinging vine:
Dependence will lead to nought.
Take note of the dodder plants
Clinging to the brushwoods and brambles.
Brushwoods and brambles thicken easily;   5
Birds clamor above and foxes burrow below;
Foxes and hares rush through left and right.
When woodcutters fell the trees
All the vines and creepers go with them.
A life of shady obscurity: 10
Meeting death with infamy and shame.
The cassia shows in the moon,
Coral grows on rocks;
The falcon flies over the ocean for food;
The dragon soars through the blue beyond.   15
Each is endowed with its own being
And is not bound up with another.
What clings together,
But thorny brambles and clinging creepers?
                                              (*YSCCC* 1/3)

The moral of "The Captive Rhinoceros" is self-evident. This poem reiterates the poet's own political philosophy, which is enunciated in the ten concluding lines. Although Yüan Chen's advice is intended for the ear of the sovereign Hsien-tsung, the historical event referred to in its headnote softens the bluntness of his pleas, and provides the background for which the poem was composed:

[Poem 13]

The Captive Rhinoceros[24]
(With an Introduction)

According to Li [i.e., Li Kung-ch'ui], during the twelfth year of the *chen-yüan* period [796], a rhinoceros was presented to the court of the Te-tsung emperor as a tribute from the South Seas. The animal died of hypothermia in the imperial park the following winter.

During the early years of *chien-chung*,
Elephants were freed from captivity
And sent back into the forests of the southern provinces.
Wild beasts were returned to their mountains
And birds built new nests;   5
Eagles and falcons were released.
During the *chen-yüan* period,
A rhinoceros was brought to court as tribute.
A special cage was set up in the imperial park
And an officer was charged to care for it.   10
Though fed from jade plates and gold cups,
Can the imprisoned tiger or the netted fish feed?
Orange trees transplanted north of the river
Or raccoons crossing Mount Wen:
Contrary to nature and out of season,   15
Surely they cannot survive.
So when the wintry wind from the north
Brought hoarfrost and heavy snow
The huddled body of the scaly beast stiffened.
After an endless journey and transported from port to port,   20
This marvelous creature of nature met its untimely end.

Treating a beast is similar to treating men—
One need not shower gifts on everyone;
Not to disrupt their lives is to give them rights,
Not to take what they have is better than giving rewards.   25

Rather than taking off your coat to clothe others
Or giving up your own dish to feed them,
Let husbands till and wives weave.
The people in the time of Yao did not know of Emperor Yao,
Yet they enjoyed peace, leisure, and sang the *Chi-yang*.   30
First note the elephant and then the rhinoceros;
Governing should be as easy as pointing to the palm.

(YSCCC 24/307)

D. Philosophical Discourse

Some of Yüan Chen's poems bear no specific political message, but enunciate certain of his own philosophic attitudes. Though a typical Confucian scholar, Yüan Chen had great appreciation and tolerance for Buddhist and Taoist philosophies and was well read in both. He was less tolerant, however, of folk superstition, witchcraft, and shamanism which were prevalent in his time. "The Witch of Hua" (*Hua-chih-wu*) may be taken on the literal level as a poem exposing the deceitful claims of witches or shamans who declare themselves to be mediums between gods and men. But the role of the medium also provides a ready parallel with the court eunuchs who set themselves up as intermediaries between loyal ministers and their sovereign.

[Poem 14]

The Witch of Hua[25]

Someone stood by the idol of a god:
Somber was the temple, silent was the god.
"The god is silent, what can be done?
I wish to see the god, is there a way?"

A witch came forth and asked for my gold: 5
"Access to the god is in my hands:
I alone can have audience with him;
He will not talk but through my mouth.
If you want the god to keep you safe,
Offer me money and buy me wine.   10
The god's plate is kept in my house,
Take your offerings there and you will be safe;
Or else you will meet trouble wherever you go—
By land, your carriage will break down,
By sea, storms will wreck your ship."   15

Hearing this I heaved a deep, deep sigh:
How can a just god bully an upright man?
With you blocking the road, who dares go south or north?
You forge god's words and abuse his power.
If the god does not know that his power is abused,   20
Those who follow his way will not be saved.
I want to see a god rid of witches,
And not seek his blessings through a witch.
O Witch! O witch!
Are you the only one who has not heard: 25
"Rather than courting mysteries,
Court your own stove.
I will drive my carriage along the road.
O witch! keep yourself to your own good.
In my heart are the canon prayers of Confucius."   30
                            (*YSCCC* 25/325–26)

The ancient Chinese saying, "Man's way is short; heaven's
way is long," is comparable but not identical to the common
English adage, "Man proposes; God disposes." In the long
philosophical poem that follows, Yüan Chen develops humanist
ideals and argues that perhaps conventional views are not always
correct views, i.e., the way of man is *not* always short and man
in many ways may overcome his shortcomings.

[Poem 15]
Man's Way is Short[26]

The ancients say man's way is short, heaven's way is long,
But I say, heaven's way is short, man's way is long.
It is heaven's way to revolve night and day ceaselessly;
Spring, fall, winter, and summer hurry along;
Wild are the winds, rain storms, thunder, and lightning.   5
Clouds darken the bright sky,
The moon steals the luster of sunlight;
Granted there are constellations and stars,
And the constant splendor of the sun.

Truly heaven controls life,   10
But virtue is the strength of men.
Yao and Shun were sage kings,
Yet heaven did not allow them to reign forever.

Their gold scepters and jade insignia
Were transferred to the First Emperor of Ch'in.   15
Why can Duke Chou and Fu Yüeh not be ministers forever?
Why did Lao-tzu and Confucius wander about in their times?
The rustic and the refined, of stations low and high,
Cannot enjoy but a few decades.

What if they were happily married and rich like Liang Chi,   20
Who lived in pomp and glory for a time?
For such contradictory affairs
Is it not because heaven's way is short,
Or is it because heaven's way is long?

Yao and Shun left their divine legacy   25
So that hundreds of dynasties to come might benefit.
Confucius taught filial piety,
So that for centuries fathers and sons dare not destroy each other.
After the Master had been dead for a millenium,
The T'ang emperor canonized him as Prince of Letters.   30
Lao-tzu left five thousand words
Transmitted to millions in posterity.
During the holy rule of T'ang
He was posthumously titled: King of the Primal Mystery,
While his soul resides in the heavenly court.   35

The twenty *chüan* of the *Rites of Chou*
Will bring order to the state for those who put them to use.
Fu Yüeh's *Discourse* contains only three or four pages;
He who masters it will be the master of the world.

Heaven can control the life of man,   40
But there is no end to men's ways.
To reckon their wondrous deeds,
Who can say that man's way is short?
Is man's way not really long?

Heaven can grow hundreds of plants: 45
The stench of the *yu* plant lasts as long as ten years,
The fragrant hibiscus blooms but a single day.
Yet men can make perfume out of lilacs, myrrh, and orchids.
Heaven knows how to breed birds and beasts
And feed tigers, leopards, and wolves;   50
But men can brew liquor out of seeds, grains, or roots,
And pour libations and cook savory dishes.

The cuckoo does not last a hundred years;
Heaven allows all fowls to feed their young,
Except for the phoenix.   55
Huge boas live for a thousand years,
Filling their bellies with cattle and elephants.
Crocodiles and serpents have their mutations,
Evil spirits and monsters, their concealment,
Mosquitoes, their sharp suckers,   60
Brambles and nettles, their thorns.
It is man's way to distinguish and discriminate.
Faith in heaven's way is foolishness,
In the face of such confusing matters
Is it not that heaven's way is short and man's way long? 65
                              (*YSCCC* 23/289–91)

We have seen in "The Captive Rhinoceros" a hint of the Taoist
philosophy of laissez-faire, or letting things take their own
course, in Yüan Chen's political thought. This idea is more
concretely expressed in the next poem, in which he advocates
the philosophy of not doing violence against nature or natural
ways. Peaceful coexistence is possible only if individual living
things are allowed to develop according to their own nature.
He also seems to be saying that certain individual experiences
cannot be shared, and that empathy cannot be complete without
common experiences.

[Poem 16]
                        Do Not Fault

          Birds do not know how to walk,
              Beasts do not know how to fly—
          One knows not the other,
              How can each hold the other to scorn?

          Dogs drink no dew,   5
              Cicadas eat no flesh—
          Try to change their diet:
              The cicada will die, the dog will starve.

          Swallows rest on beams,
              Mice nest behind stairs—   10
          To each his own dwelling;
              Man cannot change it.

> Women are skilled at needlework,
>> Men delight in the classics;
> The male begets, the female weds—   15
>> They share no common knowledge.
>
> Sensing my deafness, you cup your ear;
>> Feeling your pain, I knit my brows.
> I do not fault you—
>> Do not fault me.   20

(*YSCCC* 23/288–89)

II *Poems of a Personal Nature*

Although Yüan Chen prided himself on being a didactic poet and placed high value on his poems that carried social significance, he wrote many poems of a personal nature which are, for the most part, more lively and more appealing. Since he was such a prolific poet and wrote on a very wide range of subjects, by way of contrast I shall select a few of those poems that most readily express his intimate personal feelings, and group them thematically under a) friendship and parting, b) personal romance, and c) elegiac songs.

A. Friendship and Parting

Friendship has almost always been an important theme for Chinese poets, and it takes on particular significance in the life of Yüan Chen. Despite the many adverse criticisms intimated and leveled against him by his enemies regarding his dubious character and his political ambitions, Yüan Chen was capable of establishing long and lasting relationships with men of impeccable personal integrity and public respect. His friendship with Po Chü-i, in particular, has been recognized as "a sort of national institution";[27] widely celebrated in his own lifetime, it still remains the most memorable relationship in the literary history of China. Indeed, Yüan Chen is today more frequently remembered as the closest friend of Po Chü-i than as a celebrated T'ang poet in his own right.

This lifelong friendship between Yüan Chen and Po Chü-i, which began in 802 when they passed the placing examinations together, continued unaltered for thirty years until Yüan Chen's

death in 831.[28] It was natural that a strong bond should be
established between the two, since they not only shared a
similar social background and political ideology, but also a common view on the nature and function of literature. Their mutual
admiration and their friendly spirit of rivalry served to stimulate
the literary activities of both men, and the literary criticism exchanged between them enhanced the development of their poetic
skills. Actually the time the two spent together was rather
limited, but their close friendship was due not so much to days
spent together as to regular poetic exchanges during long periods
of separation. They composed poems with and to each other
when they were together; they carried on their correspondence
in verse when they .were apart. In 810, shortly after he was
banished to Chiang-ling, Yüan Chen received a long poem
entitled "A Hundred Rhymes as a Substitute for a Letter" from
Po Chü-i, to which he responded in kind, using the same
rhyme words in the same sequence as they appeared in Po's
poem (i.e., *tz'u-yün*). In his poem Yüan Chen reviews their
friendship from their early days in Ch'ang-an, when they were
fellow students. He likens their relationship to:

[Poem 17]
.   .   .   .
The loosened thoroughbred took its first flight,
The unfettered falcon soared from its captor's glove.
Speeding ahead, we feared earth might be too narrow;
Looking upward we felt heaven could be too low.
.   .   .   .

(*YSCCC* 10/124)

In the same poem Yüan Chen recalls that in an earlier exchange
of poems he compared Po to a "resting phoenix," and that his
friend in turn likened him to "an ancient well." He also speaks
of their sharing each other's views and ideas, and stimulating
each other's creativity:

.   .   .   .
Expanding our knowledge, we derived mutual benefit;
Culling the best, each saw a mentor in the other.

Shedding the hackneyed and the vulgar, we invented new songs;
Perfecting our craftsmanship, we reached and made great progress.
. . . .

(*Ibid.*)

There follow other reminiscences of excursions together, their
studying together for the final palace examination, and Yüan
Chen's own assignment to imperial censor following the successful passing of the examination. Later, he cites reasons for
his own banishment to the provinces. Since a poem of such
length inevitably lapses into the prosaic in places, only eight
lines have been translated. Some shorter poems Yüan Chen
wrote to Po Chü-i (i.e., Lo-t'ien) between 810 and 820, when
Yüan Chen was mostly in the provinces, are given in full.

[Poem 18]

To Lo-t'ien

From dusk till dawn I sit idly thinking of you,
Recalling events of the past doubles my sadness;
Since we took our examinations together our hearts have
  beat in unison.
When we received our first office we were still beardless.
After twenty years' exposure to the ways of the world,   5
I end up a thousand miles away in this old river town.
There ought yet to be a road ahead of me,
But who knows where on earth it will lead?

(*YSCCC* 22/272)

[Poem 19]

Thanking Lo-t'ien for Dreaming of Me

The thousandfold mountains and rivers obstruct news from
  each other;
Caring so, you saw me frequently in your dreams.
Recent illness has perverted my soul—
I only dream of persons of no concern, rarely of you.

(*YSCCC* 20/256)

[Poem 20]
To Lo-t'ien on the Twenty-fourth Day of the Third Month While
Staying at Ts'eng-feng Lodge at Night, Watching the *Wu-t'ung*
Blossom.[29]

A faint moon shines upon the *wu-t'ung* blossom;
The moonlight is pale, the flowers blurry.
O how the melancholy surroundings pain me.
Pacing to and fro, I brush aside the window curtains.
New leaves cast slender shadows,   5
Dew is heavy upon frail branches;
The longer the night, the deeper my spring grief.
A clear wind brings a faint fragrance;
Tonight far, far away I miss you especially.
Since our parting I am emaciated as a skeleton.   10
I only regret that the times are out of joint,
I withhold my judgment over the good or evil in government.
Sending memorials to the Golden Imperial Hall,
You tread the floor of the Green Dragon Palace.
I am at a lodging in these mountains,   15
The ground is covered with *wu-t'ung* blossoms.

                                        (*YSCCC* 6/65–66)

[Poem 21]
                        Transplanting Bamboo[30]
                        (With an Introduction)

Earlier Lo-t'ien sent me a poem containing the lines, "Rippleless
the water in the ancient well,/ Full of nodes the autumn bamboo."
This autumn, as I transplanted the bamboo in the courtyard in front
of my window, I commit my thoughts to these rhymes to him.

Once you noted my upright nature
And likened me to the autumn bamboo.
Autumn has now intensified my longing for you.
Missing you, I transplanted the bamboo close to my window.
Removed from their native soil their colors have changed;   5
With injured roots, their sparse leaves
Rustle sadly in the slightest breeze.
On their round trunks, half bare, all nodes are shown.

The sounds of cicadas cover the evening;
Leaping frogs gather about the balustrade in the dusk.   10
Night and day, dust collects in the air,
Clear skies are hidden beyond the haze.
Tan-ch'iu, the fairyland, is too far away,
How can I ever hope to reach its holy altar?
The humid air by the river keeps the grass green in winter, 15

So that one is not aware when autumn ends.
I pity the towering bamboo:
Each bare trunk, a staff of jade.
But the solitary phoenix will never come—
Alone, I grieve over the passing of the year.

(*YSCCC* 2/18–19)

This poem may refer to an actual act of transplanting the bamboo, as the poet claims in the headnote. But that Po Chü-i earlier in a poem to him compared him to the bamboo, so cherished by the recipient, seems to have been ignored by Yüan Chen's detractors when they criticized his moral character. The bamboo is a traditional symbol for Confucian scholar-officials, for the Chinese character *chieh*, which I translate as "nodes" on the bamboo, also means "integrity" and "chastity" in the moral sense. The last two lines are in particular rich with symbolism. On the literal level, the bamboo's nodes are more visible because it is stripped of leaves. On the metaphorical level, the poet's personal integrity becomes more evident by virtue of his being deprived of the flourishing signs of rank and influence. The double entendre of *chieh* is clearly implied by the mention of the "bare trunk." The bamboo is said to be the only tree besides the *wu-t'ung* tree that the phoenix will rest on. Since Yüan Chen had earlier likened Po Chü-i to a "resting phoenix," these lines may also describe Yüan Chen's personal disappointment at not being able to have his friend visit him.

[Poem 22]
Responding to Lo-t'ien for Remembering Me in Early Summer[31]

The orange tree in the courtyard is drooping with fruit,
The swallow's nest is empty of young birds.
I also am a swallow; having left my nest,
I feel just as lost and forlorn.
Your verse speaks of the early summer;   5
I sigh for the advent of autumn.
The food and conditions are all so strange here,
The weather, too, is so different from ours,
Wild weeds cover the rice fields.
I have moved to live by the river.   10

On the eighth and ninth of the month
Moonlight partially invades the night.

(*YSCCC* 6/67)

After approximately five years in Chiang-ling, Yüan Chen was
recalled to Ch'ang-an for a new assignment. He had a reunion
with Po Chü-i and other old friends for a brief period, during
which time they composed a good number of light verses that
Yüan Chen called *yen-tz'u* (romantic songs). In the spring of
815 Yüan left the capital once more for his new post as marshal
of T'ung-chou. While en route he sent Po Chü-i a poem in
response to the latter's earlier farewell poem:

[Poem 23]

Response to Lo-t'ien Drunk at Parting

Last time I left we were parted for five years.
Who knows how long this parting will be!
Adieu, Lo-t'ien! Do not be depressed—
Suppose I had not come back to Ch'ang-an at all.

(*YSCCC* 20/255)

T'ung-chou (modern Ta-hsien in Szechwan) is located in a
valley on the northwestern bank of the river Chu, about 140
miles northeast of Chungking. The high humidity in that region
was believed to be conducive to malaria. The new assignment
for Yüan Chen, whose title remained "marshal," meant being
farther away from home and civilization. A sense of irony
invests the following poem:

[Poem 24]

T'ung-chou

All my life I have desired to live in the mountains—
The skies of T'ung-chou are enclosed by peaks.
Having nothing to do all day, I sleep till sundown,
And I am paid thirty thousand cash per month for doing nothing.

(*YSCCC* 20/252)

Shortly after his arrival, he contracted malaria and was
seriously ill for months. The most moving poem he sent to Po

Chü-i is perhaps the following quatrain (written after he received news that his friend, too, had been banished from the capital to Chiang-chou, Chiu-chiang), which is heavily charged with emotion and pathos:

[Poem 25]

On Hearing of Lo-t'ien's Banishment to Chiang-chou

The flickering flame of the lamp casts ghostly shadows
Tonight when I heard you were banished to Chiu-chiang.
Nearing death on my sickbed, I started in disbelief;
The dreary wind blasted cold rain through my window.

(*YSCCC* 20/249)

Po Chü-i was so moved by this poem that, on his way to Chiang-ling, he dispatched several poems to Yüan Chen. The following is one of the three poems Yüan wrote in reply:

[Poem 26]

Thanking Lo-t'ien for Sending Me Three Poems While En Route to Chiang-chou (verse 3)

Other people, too, have friends they love,
But our friendship differs from all others.
Each day I would rather forego food and drink;
My only wish is to be with you.
If one day we did not meet,   5
I would sit sadly, my soul locked in darkness.
Imagine how hard for us now to live without each other;
Like two cloud clusters we have drifted ten thousand miles apart.
The clouds above are at the whim of strong winds,
Their meetings are difficult to predict.   10
If obstacles exist even in heaven,
What are the chances for men on earth?

(*YSCCC* 8/91)

[Poem 27]

Learning of Lo-t'ien Reading My Poems At Night on the River

I heard that you were moored on the western bank one night
And chanted my poems till daybreak.
Tonight in T'ung-chou I also cannot sleep;
The mountain is full of wind and rain and cuckoo calls.

(*YSCCC* 21/260)

[Poem 28]
   Thanking Lo-t'ien for Sending Poems to Comfort Me During
My Illness

Twisting and turning, where does the road to the future lead?
Growing old, how can I not be despondent?
Fearing the wind in my illness, I remain in bed for months,
Sitting up only to watch the flowers or take medicine.
Enclosed and shut in amid stagnant air I have lost all companions.   5
Mounting waves in the channel obstruct the view of my homeland.
Only two streams of tears are left this autumn
To greet your new poems sent from far away.

                                        (*YSCCC* 21/264)

[Poem 29]
           To Lo-t'ien for Sending a Verse in the Spring

   The parrot is smart, the sparrow dense;
   But why are they both trapped in the cage?
   To avoid the whale, you are caught in perilous waves;
   Daring to chase the serpent, I am lost in a malarial fog.
   A thousand mountains between us, our communication is
           interrupted: 5
   Far apart, we share the spring fete marked on the calendar.
   A tree of plum blossoms, several cups of wine—
   When I get drunk I search for you on the river bank and
           weep to the east wind.

                                        (*YSCCC* 21/260)

[Poem 30]
                   Responding to Lo-t'ien's Verse Written
                   On the Third Day of the Third Month

   On this day once we got drunk before the blossoms.
   Today, before the blossoms, I am all alone.
   Leaning against the worn curtain, I idly stare—
   A pity that the beauty of springtime is wasted here.
                                        (*YSCCC* 21/260)

[Poem 31]
                           To Lo-t'ien[32]

   Don't grieve over my growing old in the western wilderness,
   Hui-chi is actually a scenic wonder of the world.

Before Ling-fan Bridge a mirror extends for miles;
Amid the five clouds, peaks float like stone sails.
Ice melts from the field; short reeds point like awls;   5
Spring enters the branches, pussywillows burst.
Would that my old friend had wings
So he could fly here and get drunk with me.

> (*YSCCC* 22/274–75)

[Poem 32]

To Lo-t'ien

Don't say it is easy to cross the boundary that separates
     our neighboring districts;
With each of us helplessly tied to his post, what can we do?
The older we grow, the harder to part again,
For the white-haired ones, the span of life shrinks fast.

> (*YSCCC* 22/270)

Po Chü-i kept in his household several singers and musicians.
Among them was one called Ling-lung, who could sing dozens
of Yüan Chen's poems. When Yüan Chen visited Po Chü-i's
district during one of his own inspection tours, Po Chü-i en-
tertained his guest by having Ling-lung sing at the party. On
hearing his own poems sung by the girl, Yüan Chen wrote this
short poem:

[Poem 33]

Parting Again

Don't let Ling-lung sing my verse,
My verse is mostly about our partings.
Tomorrow morning we will again part at the head of the river,
When the moon sets and the tide goes out.

> (*YSCCC* 22/271)

The two friends met for the last time in 829, when Yüan Chen
visited Po Chü-i in Lo-yang on his way from Yüeh-chou to the
capital. The following are the last two poems he wrote to Po
Chü-i before they took leave of each other. These are the only
poems by Yüan Chen written after 825 that have been preserved,

because they were included in Po Chü-i's "Memorial Address to Yüan Chen's Soul."[33]

[Poem 34]

Words of Sorrow

(1)

Don't chide me for lingering here so long:
However hard I try, I cannot bring myself to say goodbye.
Let me tarry a little longer, white-haired friends are getting fewer;
Tomorrow you may not have the pleasure of my company again.

[Poem 35]

(2)

Since we became friends, three long separations we have endured.
When we met this last time my beard, too, had turned white.
I found it hard to part, you ought to understand:
Who can tell if we'll ever see each other again!

(*PSCCC* 60/344)

These are premonitory words. They never saw each other again. Within two years Yüan Chen died in Wu-ch'ang, on the twenty-second of the seventh month 831.

Po Chü-i was undoubtedly Yüan Chen's closest friend and rival in poetry. Po Chü-i, in a postscript to his own (second series) collection, the *Po-shih chi* in twenty-five *chüan*, mentions that seventeen *chüan* and almost a thousand poems, titled *Yüan Po ch'ang-ho yin chih chi*, contained exchange poems between himself and Yüan Chen. Unfortunately, the exact number of poems Yüan addressed to Po cannot be determined, since most of his works written after 825 have been lost.

Other than the several hundred poems he sent to Po Chü-i, Yüan Chen also carried on frequent correspondence in verse with other fellow poets. Among them were such famous names as Liu Yü-hsi (referred to as Liu Meng-te), Li Shen (i.e., Li Kung-ch'ui, nicknamed by his friends "Shorty Li"), Li Chien (also known as Li the Twelfth), Yang Chü-yüan, and Po Chü-i's brother, Po Hsing-chien, to mention but a few.

Parting with friends is one of the most moving and emotionally charged themes in Yüan's verse. Several examples are translated here.

[Poem 36]

Diverging Currents

In antiquity, tears of parting,
Drop by drop,

Formed diverging currents.
Day and night,
One current flows east,   5
The other flows west;
For thousands of miles
The two courses never meet—
Each creating its own waves.
The opposite directions   10
Remind me of these diverging currents.

(*YSCCC* 5/53)

[Poem 37]

Presenting a Cherry Blossom Branch as a Parting Gift

Seeing you off under the cherry trees
I break off the spring in my heart with a branch of cherry blossoms.
Our separation will be most keenly felt
When myriad petals fall from hundreds of cherry trees.

(*YSCCC* 18/226)

[Poem 38]

Offering Li the Twelfth a Peony Petal as a Parting Gift

The oriole's last note sounds strained;
Catkins are flying in the wind;
The peony blossoms are fading
While the leaves thrive in clumps.
Too sad to leave the scene for a whole year   5
I offer you a pink petal
By the red railing
As a parting gift.

(*YSCCC* 17/207)

[Poem 39]

Dreaming of Li Shen at Ch'ang-t'an

All alone; I went to bed
    with a thousand melancholy thoughts;

But when I closed my eyes you were there
    and we spent a lovely night together.
What a pity that only our dreaming souls
    know no distance of separation,
Nor wind nor rain can keep you from
    coming to Ch'ang-t'an.

(*YSCCC* 19/244)

[Poem 40]

Post Pavilion Moon
(With an Introduction)

At the Lo-k'ou posthouse, I saw inscribed on the wall the name of
Ts'ui the Twenty-Second. A few nights later, when I was watching
the moon from Green Hill Post, I recalled that Mr. Ts'ui was fond
of arguments based on practicality. Every time we spent the night
together he used to say, "Man should work during the day and rest
at night. To stroll idly in the moonlight is what I never do." After
saying this he would stubbornly lie down. Others could not stir
him with a hundred or a thousand words of persuasion or argument.
Remembering the past, I feel sad and at a loss. So I write this poem
to him:

You were practical and I, romantic;
We argued often about strolling in the moonlight.
Tonight at the mountain post fenced by southern cliffs
I know you are already in bed while I am strolling alone.

(*YSCCC* 17/211–12)

In his "Response to Chih-tui," Yüan Chen seems to assume
a *Ch'an* (Zen) Buddhist attitude, in which the sorrows of separation are obliterated by an act of self-discipline, which, in the
end, is also negated:

[Poem 41]

Response to Chih-tui[34]

Ultimately we must discipline ourselves to the point where
    no discipline is required,
And listen to the sound until no sound is heard.
Don't allow your heart to be consumed with longing for me;
In my own heart there is neither me nor you.

(*YSCCC* 20/251–52)

B. Romantic Poems

Many of Yüan Chen's poems written to his friends, in particular those addressed to Po Chü-i, may seem overly sentimental, almost like love poems to anyone uninformed about Chinese cultural traditions. It may be said that friendship, since the time of Confucius, has been regarded by the Chinese as one of the five human relationships to be cultivated, cherished, and respected by all civilized people.[35] Poets living according to Confucian norms were more reticent in airing their feelings about love between the sexes than in writing about their deep attachments for friends of the same sex. When Yüan Chen's critics called him "frivolous," they had in mind not his sentimental poems on friendship, but the type of poems which he himself labeled "romantic poems" (*yen-tz'u*), and which he stated numbered more than one hundred when he divided his poetry collection into ten categories in 812. These so-called romantic poems, however, were omitted from subsequent editions of his *Collected Works*, possibly by well-meaning editors who felt that poetry of this kind was unworthy of a Confucian scholar and sometime chief minister. Fortunately, some of the poems belonging to this group are preserved elsewhere. Fifty-seven of them found their way into the anthology *Ts'ai-tiao chi* (*Collection of Voices of Geniuses*) compiled by Wei Ku (fl. 934–965) of the Five Dynasties. Some of these poems were also included in the *Ch'üan T'ang shih* (*The Complete Poems of T'ang*) and the Japanese anthology *Senzaikaku* compiled by Oē-nō Koretoki (888–963).[36]

Because of their content, these romantic poems of Yüan Chen were perhaps not meant for public circulation. Nonetheless, they were more popular than his more serious poems of social protest. Some of these poems are simple portrayals of feminine beauty and fashion; some are about beautiful women the poet was acquainted with, including famous courtesans and sing-song girls; some are reminiscences of romantic liaisons of his youth, that hidden side of the poet's life that his detractors tended to overemphasize and his proponents tried to ignore. Most interesting of all are several poems of a confessional nature that may shed light on facts in his life that have been blurred or obliterated by the passage of time. A long poem of seventy rhymes (140 lines) entitled "Dream of a Spring Excursion" is worth reading for biographical data if for nothing else. Even though the poem is not included in his *Collected Works,* that Yüan Chen was its real author can be verified by Po Chü-i, whose own *Collected Works* contains a poem bearing the same title of Yüan Chen's poem.[37] But instead of the original seventy rhymes, Po's poem consists of a hundred rhymes—besides reiterating the original themes in Yüan Chen's poem, Po Chü-i used sixty extra lines exhorting his friend to free himself from the snares of the world such as love, honors, and worldly success and to turn to Buddhism, which alone could lead to enlightenment and eternal salvation. Moreover, in the introductory note prefacing the poem, Po Chü-i states: "Wei-chih [Yüan Chen] sent me *his* poem, "Dream of a Spring Excursion in Seventy Rhymes," upon his arrival at Chiang-ling. In his letter accompanying the poem he entreats me saying, 'These words should not be made known to those who do not know me. Yet [I feel] the knowledge of my experience must be shared with someone who knows me. You, Lo-t'ien, of all my friends know me best. How dare I not make it known to you?'. . ."[38]

Yüan Chen's own poem can be roughly divided into three sections. The first section, consisting of five stanzas (stanza divisions have been adopted for the sake of convenience, although the original shows no formal breaks in structure, and breaks are indicated only by changes in the rhyme patterns), takes up the theme embodied in the title. It unfolds in suggestive language a romantic encounter with a fairylike woman in the framework of a dream. The second section (stanzas 6–9) describes the years that followed the dreamlike romance of his youth—a state of "reality" signified by his marriage to Wei Hui-ts'ung (or Ch'eng-chih), whose death seems to end the springtime of his own life. The reference to a *yüeh-fu* song in the last line of stanza 8 ("Why bother to compare the plain with the fancy weave?") is both pathetic and ironic. It is pathetic because in dream as well as in reality he loses both of the women he loved—his mistress as represented in the dream vision and his wife as represented in reality; ironical because in the original *yüeh-fu* song that is alluded to here the "plain weave" symbolizes the wife that is deserted, and the "fancy weave" symbolizes a new-found love.[39] In Yüan Chen's own case, however, the situation is reversed in the sense that his mistress, who is his first love, may be better likened to the "fancy weave," while his wife, his new-found love, the "plain weave." The poet seems to realize the irony in comparing his own foibles with those of his prototype; and the pathos is intensified with the disillusioning words "why bother," since, *vanitas vanitatum*, in the end he is left with nothing. The third section (stanzas 10–11) is a recapitulation, this time in terms of his lofty ambitions and political setbacks. The poem ends on a note of self-vindication, translated into the poetic image of a lotus leaf, a symbol of purity amidst contamination.

[Poem 42]
Dream of a Spring Excursion[40]

Once I dreamt of an excursion in spring:
In the spring excursion what did I see?
I dreamt I entered a deep, deep cavern
Where I fulfilled my life-long wish:

Cool and clear flows the shallow stream.   5
In a painted boat with magnolia oars
I drift by a myriad blooming peach trees,
By a winding path lined with bamboo,
A long veranda embracing a tiny house
With doors and windows on both sides.   10
Below the house grows a variety of flowers,
At the edge of the flowerbeds egrets circle;
A pool reflects the colors of the sky
Before the rise of the morning sun.

Not daring to climb straight up the steps,   15
I tiptoe lightly along the curved pool.
The Black Dragon makes no sound;
Pi-yü is the object of my longing.
By and by I arrive between the curtain and the door;
Being apprehensive, I hesitate before entering.   20
I peep into the rooms to the east and to the west;
Everywhere objets d'art are tastefully arrayed.
The partitions are lacquered green,
The camel-bone hooks are painted red-gold.
As the sun rises higher and higher   25

There are signs and sounds of people stirring.
The parrot, hungry, cries out raucously;
The lap dog shows anger even in slumber.
The curtain lifted, a girl-servant appears;
Seeing me, she seems to understand without words.   30

A red embroidered coverlet is spread over the mat,
Jewelry lies scattered on the dressing table;
Quietly I lift the kingfisher bedcurtain
And gaze upon her coral loveliness.
Before I recognize her flowerlike person,   35
I am intoxicated by her sweet fragrance.
As she turns, her white nightdress slides to one side,
Revealing her curves—a cluster of morning clouds;
Her face in slumber—a budding peach blossom
      burst open by the wind;
In perspiration, she is a flower decked with dew.   40

Her hair is styled in a hundred-leaved coiffure;
Her gold slippers are of double platform soles.
Her soft silk skirt is threaded with gold;
Her pantaloons are of a print of mimosa patterns.
Dazzling in beauty, her makeup has faded;   45
Next to her all the garments look dull and worn.
A red peony, she is in full bloom,
Awakened by the rain at the end of spring.

The dreaming soul was easily startled;
In the immortal realm I could not tarry long.   50
Night after night I stared at the Sky River,
But there was no way to retrace my steps.
Focusing my thoughts on what the heart desires
Is to acquire sudden enlightenment.
Having been enlightened, for eight or nine years   55
I never dallied among the flowers,
Though I lived through springtime at both capitals,
Amid the clamor and chatter of flocks of birds.

When it is time for me to enjoy the flowers
I only write verse in memory of the immortal.   60
In this floating life, all those past experiences
Exist to confirm my moral steadfastness.
Even now I write poems about her in my dream.

I alone know how taxing it has been on my emotions.
A dream after all must not be taken too seriously.   65
So in time I was married to another.

At the time I was twenty-four.
The feast lasted long, long into the night.
Morning hibiscus with jade pendants bid me welcome.
A tall pine in strength is the beautiful Lo-fu.   70
The Wei House was in its full glory;
At home or stepping out, we shared great joy.
By the grand mansion the clear pool was full;
The neighboring ponies pulled our scarlet coach.
In the spacious ballroom, dances were often held;   75
At the long banquet tables, celebrities gathered.

The green spring, how many days has it in store?
In glossy fruit are hidden deadly worms.
The autumn moon yet shines upon Master P'an;
An empty mound encloses Tutor Hsieh.   80
The red mansion has become crumbled walls;
The Gold Valley is lost in growing thickets.
Stones lay in heaps on the ruined balustrade;
Doors lean against the old stockades.
Dreams and reality are directly opposed,   85
But alike are they in impermanency.
How do I describe my present state of mind?
An entangled skein of silk hard to unravel.
Lady Cho and her "White Hair Song,"
Ah Chiao and the "Gold Chamber *fu*,"   90
The double-decked jade tower of Shen-chi,
The evergreen tomb of Ming-fei:
All came to the same end—their bones turned to dust,
Flowed into streams that pour into the sea.
Since the past was no different from the present,   95
Why bother to compare the plain with the fancy weave?

When I was in the glow of my glory,
My goal in life was set at an early age.
Singled out to head the sage and the able,
I dared to counsel on good and evil.   100
At thirty, once more I returned to court;
The ascent was followed by another fall.
Favors and honors were bestowed upon me in my prime,

Setbacks have also been frequently met.
The spirit of directness is in my vitals;   105
It grows worse like a chronic illness.
Not to speak out is to be unhappy [with myself];
To speak frankly my words are obstinate—
Obstinacy is what most people abhor;
But my nature is also endowed by God.   110
I would rather be an aloe sinking beneath the water
Than floating on the surface like a gourd.
Truly I have kept my integrity firm,
Though I have not been circumspect in my action.
Event after event I have experienced,   115
To and fro I ponder on where I went wrong.

Fine jade is chiseled into insignia of rank;
Good metal is forged into arms for the arsenal.
I only know how to keep myself steadfast and pure
Not expecting that I should be shaped and tempered!   120
A long rope to lasso the wild horse,
A mesh net to trap the hare in hiding;
Beyond the reaches of this mad world,
Who can restrain me from far away?
Opportunity comes and goes, flitting;   125
Calamity strikes with great speed.
Since I was not wise in past actions,
What is there to say about my present trip?
I shall make a good effort in Chiang-ling,
But with whom can I share a chat or a joke?   130
The river flowers here may be lovely,
But they are not what my heart desires.
Carnations may boast of their craftiness,
Turnips may brag of covering the acres—
All are products of poor soil;   135
Deep or shallow they are unworthy of my envy!
The lotus leaf growing from the water,
Round and full it dwells in the stream.
If you pour water over it—
Lo, it is neither stained nor sullied.   140

(*TTC* 5/56–57)

Po Chü-i's own poem harmonizing with Yüan Chen's "Dream of a Spring Excursion," sixty lines longer than Yüan Chen's, is a reiteration or elaboration on the same theme—grieving over his friend's misfortune in politics as well as in private life. What Po added is a plea for his friend to turn to Buddhism for spiritual consolation and salvation by disengaging himself from the snares of worldly attachment. Although Po Chü-i showed his own Buddhist faith in his poetry, Yüan Chen seemed to be just as well-versed in rudimentary Buddhist philosophy. In a poem harmonizing with Po's poem to a *Ch'an* (Zen) master named Yün Chi, Yüan Chen retorts in similar Buddhist terminology:

[Poem 43]
If you hope to rid the three thousand realms of worry,
Don't knock at the *Ch'an* gate with the eighty myriad rules.
The flame in your heart, self-ignited, must die of its own accord,
Master Yün Chi has no way to put it out for you.

(YSCCC 19/243)

In the long confessional poem, "Dream of a Spring Excursion," Yüan Chen tells of the two tragedies in his private life: the termination of a passionate *affaire de coeur* in his youth (like a "dream"), and the end of a happy marriage by the death of his first wife ("reality"). The grief over the loss of his wife is shown in a series of elegiac poems that will be discussed in the following pages. Lingering memories of the object of his premarital liaison also inspired many other poems that Yüan Chen labeled as "romantic" (*yen-shih*). Could the "jadelike person" in the following poem, "The White Gown," be the same young woman?

[Poem 44]
The White Gown[41]

The light dust is sprinkled by a light rain;
A waft of fragrance drifts across the thin wall.
The jadelike person has just slipped into her white gown:
Gazing on her embroidery in a melancholy air,
She is a pear blossom against the ivory couch.

Her lavender silk blouse and willow green skirt
Are being scented by slow smoldering aloes.
I lean against the screen and laugh at Chou Fang—
What a waste of energy to paint morning clouds?

(TTC 5/60)

The white gown seems to have held some special significance for Yüan Chen's romantic past; possibly it was a nightgown his mistress wore during their first secret meeting. It is referred to again in the poem "Peach Blossoms":

[Poem 45]
> A myriad shades of peach blossoms
> Correspond to the rouge and powder on her cheeks.
> The spring breeze assists in breaking my heart
> By blowing the petals from her white gown.
>
> (*TTC* 5/59)

Among the romantic poems of Yüan Chen there are two courting poems entitled "Spring Songs." They could very well be the two "Spring Songs" mentioned but not included in "The Story of Ying-ying." In the story the protagonist, Scholar Chang, sends to Ying-ying through her maidservant, Hung-niang, two poems with the same title.

[Poem 46]
Spring Songs[42]

I

> Since spring I have been drawn to the east of Sung Yü's house.
> Trailing my sleeves and loosening my collar, I await a favorable wind.
> The oriole is in hiding in the willow's gloom, no one is about;
> Only a tree of pink blossoms tints the wall.
>
> (*CTShih* 422/4644)

[Poem 47]
II

> Deep in the deserted garden, the trees and grass are lush;
> Coy oriole is silent, hidden in retreat.
> Idly she steers the drifting petals in the stream
> To flow beyond the gate to tease Master Jüan.
>
> (*CTShih* 422/4644)

"Oriole" (i.e., "Ying-ying") also appears as the title of a poem that seems to refer to his first meeting with the girl (a parallel but more detailed description of a similar meeting between Chang and Ying-ying is found in the short story).

[Poem 48]

Oriole

Dark red and light green were the colors of her dress,
Careless was her coiffure, faded her makeup—
Lotus wrapt in mist, kissed by the glow of dawn;
Peony drenched with rain, weeping at the setting sun.

Was there a fleeting smile, or no smile at all?   5
Her fragrance I smelt was not that of perfume.
In outrage, her sparkling eyes blazed at her mother
For urging her to greet a young swain.

(CTShih 422/4642)

The following poem, "A Secret Letter" (*Yü-chung shu*, literally, "Letter Inside a Fish"), again seems to have reference to Yüan Chen's famous prose romance, which contains an exceedingly moving letter from the heroine, Ying-ying, to the protagonist, Scholar Chang. Could that famous letter be the subject of this poem?

[Poem 49]

A Secret Letter

I fold and unfold her letter;
Unconsciously my hands spread it open again.
Amid tear stains a trace of rouge runs across the page—
The letter paper must have touched her cheek.

(CTShih 122/4639–40)

Granted there is no definite proof that these poems were written about the heroine of Yüan's love story or about any other young woman in the poet's life, yet they are of interest because they shed some light on the dark secret of Yüan Chen's private life and present us with a glimpse of the man in his unguarded moments.

A better known and more admired poem in this group is perhaps the frequently anthologized piece "Thoughts During Separation," about which critics never seem to be able to agree as to the addressee. Some insist that the poem was addressed to his first wife; others, to his mistress.[43] I am more inclined to

agree with the latter interpretation, because the poem echoes
and reinforces the same sentiment expressed in stanza six of
the "Dream" (poem 42) quoted earlier.

[Poem 50]
Thoughts During Separation

> Having seen the sea, I crave no other waters;
> Aside from those by Mount Wu, there is no cloud.
> I move through flower groves, casting no second glance—
> Partly because of self-discipline, partly because of you.
> (CTShih 422/4643)

Both the tone and the mood of the poem suggest a passionate
romance. The reference to Mount Wu, literally, the "Witch
Mountain" (the highest peak of the Pa range running from
Szechwan to Hupei, north of the Yangtze River), which derives
its name from its shape, contains a sexual implication, since it
alludes to Sung Yü's (fl. third century B.C.) famous *Kao-t'ang fu,*
which describes the romantic encounter of Hsiang Wang, king
of Ch'u, with the goddess of Mount Wu in a dream. Hence
the terms *Kao-t'ang, Wu shan,* and the "rain and clouds," may
all have sexual connotations. Be that as it may, one has no way
of knowing the real identity of the young lady in question. In
spite of endless speculation, she must remain an enigma, like
the "dark lady" in Shakespeare's life. Whether she was in real
life a distant cousin of the protagonist (i.e., the author), as
she is described as being in the supposedly autobiographical
story, or a lowly courtesan, as has been suggested by Ch'en
Yin-k'o,[44] she must have completely captivated the youthful
Yüan Chen so that the romance left an indelible impression on
his poetry. Reminiscences of those stolen moments together
are recorded in such verses as the following.

[Poem 51]
Dreaming of the Past

> Ennui; by the window, I relive a deep, deep dream—
> A dream I can share with no one—
> Of midnight trysts,
> And partings at dawn.

Mountains and rivers had cut us asunder;   5
Long gone was my hope for clouds and rain.
What makes me dream of you today?
It only renews the pain of separation.

(*TTC* 5/57)

[Poem 52]

Spring Dawn

Half of the sky is dawning, half is still dark.
Drunk with the scent of flowers, I imagined I heard an oriole;
And the little dog stirred at the sound of the temple bell—
I relived the feeling of two decades ago.

(*TTC* 5/60)

There is no question about Yüan Chen's infatuation with the recurrent figure of his dreams and reminiscences, but one cannot help wondering what the real reason was for his having given her up. Was he really so driven by worldly ambition that he forsook his first love in order to conclude a socially and politically advantageous marriage alliance, as Ch'en Yin-k'o has claimed? Or was it really due to the moral scruples of a Confucian, as posited by the protagonist of the story? Could it have been a feeling of a personal inadequacy and an inferiority complex in his male role, as implied by James R. Hightower?[45] Rather than speculate on these possibilities, let us try to piece together the clues given in the following "Poems of Final Farewell," a three poem cycle.

In these three verses, the first may be written from the girl's point of view; the second, the poet's; and the third may be interpreted as a dialogue or, rather, an argument between the two. The psychological factors that caused the final break are clearly stated. It seems that the poet, who admitted to being the girl's first love, was fearful that he might not be her last. The girl, on the other hand, wanted to have from him a permanent commitment he was not willing to make.

[Poem 53]

Poems of Final Farewell[46]
(In the Ancient Style)

I

I wish we were the stars—
The Cowherd and the Weaving Maid in the skies above,

And not the red hibiscus in the courtyard.
Though the stars meet once a year on the Double Seventh,
They remain constant to each other in their hearts,   5
Unlike the fickle flowers which bloom in the morn,
    but are gone at dusk,
East, west, south, or north, at the wind's will,
Once separated, the flowers keep no faith with each other.
It grieves me that our love does not last—
I feel so when we are together,   10
How much worse when we are apart!

The spring wind disturbs me, so do the shrikes' shrieks.
For this is the season you will desert me.
Clasping your hand, I entreat you for a pledge,
But you make no mention of our future together.   15
Since you are resolute to sever relations,
My own feelings are confused and distraught.
If your parting is as final as between life and death,
Should I forever live to grieve my loss?

[Poem 54]

II

O the spring ice is melting away,
My breast alone is still congealed.
O that beautiful person
Is so far, far away.
One day without seeing her,   5
That day is as long as three autumns—
And our parting has truly been three years.

Water ripples at the slightest breeze,
Bamboo shoots, however tall, have no nodes.
Will the peach and plum blossoms in spring   10
Fail to be plucked by passers-by?
I see myself drifting like a wandering cloud;
How can I hope to find you as pure as snow?
I believe the broken mirror may be separately bright;
I see my tear stains red as blood.   15
Although no one came before me in your life,
In the end can I prevent others taking you from me?
Alas, it is all over,
The Weaving Maid bids farewell to the Cowherd,

A brief union once a year, 20
Who knows what happens on the other side of the river?

[Poem 55]

III

When we slept in each other's arms night after night,
Our secret thoughts were tightly knotted.
How can the passing of an entire year
Be expressed in a single night?
All I feel is a deep, deep yearning, 5
Unfulfilled by the pleasure of this moment.
A rainbow bridge was built before the night,
The dragon coach is waiting at dawn.
How I hate the wild magpies for being so slow!
How I detest the heavenly cock for being so punctual! 10
The sky is dawning,
The morning star has faded.
Once we part there will be another year;
How can I endure another long year?
Rather than waiting for such a distant meeting, 15
We may as well part forever as if by death.
The Lord of Heaven must be jealous of our love—
Why then does he not let us make a final break?

(*TTC* 5/57–58)

C. Elegiac Poems

If Yüan Chen was responsible for the termination of his brief romance with Ying-ying, which was to haunt him like a dream, he was certainly not responsible for the termination of his marriage, which was brought on by the death of Wei Ch'eng-chih. His wife's death came only six years after their marriage. Moreover, by the time of her death, Yüan Chen had also suffered the loss of all of their children except for one little girl. *Chüan* nine of his *Collected Works* contains only elegies or elegiac poems mourning these losses, of which thirty-three are in memory of his departed wife, Wei Ch'eng-chih.

Most of these poems are not dated. Judging by internal and external evidence, they would seem to have been composed sometime between 809 and 815, during which time his deceased spouse became the principal subject of his dreams, for there are six poems recording such dreams.

[Poem 56]

Moved by a Dream

Pacing, I mourn; sitting, I sigh—there is no end to my grief.
No trace of your shadow was shown to my soul throughout the
    past year.
Tonight in the lodging of Shang-shan I dreamt of you—
Clearly, as we were in the past, together in front of our boudoir.

                                             (*YSCCC* 9/105)

    Ch'eng-chih died on the ninth day of the seventh lunar month
in the year 809. The reason that Yüan Chen did not write of his
dreams of her until the first month of 810 is perhaps that his
sorrow was too intense during the early months of bereavement.
This is explained in the first two lines of a poem that prefaces
the collection of elegies:

[Poem 57]

Brooding at Night

Extreme emotion deprives me of dreams:
A bereft soul is too easily startled—
A gust of wind fells the half-hooked curtain;
Autumn moon fills the bed with light.
Alone I sit on the front steps gazing into space;
Sighing deeply, I pace around the trees.
A lone lute encased in the gloom
Often emits notes of discord from its broken strings.

                                           (*YSCCC* 9/102)

    At first reading, the lone lute may seem to refer to Ch'eng-
chih, who was interred on the thirteenth day of the tenth month
in 809. However, the imagery in the line that follows makes it
clear that the poet is speaking of himself, since a widower is
commonly referred to as one with "broken strings" (of harmony).

    "Three Dreams in Chiang-ling" ("*Chiang-ling san meng*") are
three separate poems written between 810 and 814, during the
poet's banishment at Chiang-ling. The first consists of fifty-six
lines and 280 characters. It is the most complex of the group
in that it is in the form of a letter addressed to his wife and is
a confession of his feelings for her. The narration of the dream

is then framed within a philosophical musing at the beginning
and conclusion of the poem.

[Poem 58]

Three Dreams in Chiang-ling[47]

I

When you were alive, we often dreamt of each other,
But did you ever share my world of dreams?
Now we are separated by death,
What hope is there for my dreaming soul?
I know it is useless to dream,   5
But for dreams, how else can we meet?
What auspicious night is this night
That you have entered my dreams again?
I dreamt that you were attired the same as before,
But your face was paler and more clouded.   10
You made no reference to your death which separates us,
Saying only that you were leaving.
Bits of sewing and needlework were strewn about;
Folded were the bedcurtains and draperies;
Tearfully you caressed our little daughter,   15
Over and over you entrusted her to me,
Saying, "She is the only child we have,
A pity that I left you with no sons.
Bear in mind her tender age:
Too young to fend off hunger and cold.   20
I know you take no pleasure in trivial matters,
And can hardly take care of yourself.
Being tied down with official duties,
Can you be free to tend to family affairs?
When other couples are separated in life,   25
Maids and servants often bully the young;
If you are home, our child will be fine,
But whom to trust when you are away?"
Saying this, you were choked with sobbing;
Listening, I, too, shed torrential tears.   30
My sorrow suddenly woke me up;
As if demented, I could not sleep or sit.
Half in moonlight, the bed was half black;
The sounds of insects moving in the deep grass.
My heart and soul were at variance: 35
Was it dream or reality—I was not clear.

Deep in thought I searched for your image
Until tears streamed to sheer exhaustion.
Our life together has ended forever,
Why do I grieve so over a dream?   40

I grieve that our little daughter you loved
Is left behind and not with me.
Ch'ang-an is as distant as the sun,
Barred by mountains, streams, and clouds.
Even if I were to grow wings,   45
Fettered, I would be caught in the net.
Tonight the tears that I shed
Are also for parting with the living.
Touched by your spirit in the Yellow Springs,
I am stirred to thinking by the stream.   50
Even this river I dare not cross at will,
Much less the boundless Yellow Springs.
What causes me to cherish such extreme thoughts?
To what purpose do I pursue such a dream?
Sitting here, I watch the dawn break;   55
The river breeze whimpers between the branches.

[Poem 59]

II

In an ancient graveyard, in a cave thirty feet deep,
There is buried a precious jade flower.
Dilapidated, the door of the mound was torn off.
On the tomb, like entangled smoke, grew the grass.
Against the mound I sat for a long while;   5
In the distance a village seemed to hold my hope.
Suddenly I awoke, the bed flooded with moonlight,
The sound of wind and waves on the river.

[Poem 60]

III

Your bones have long turned to dust
And my heart is already dead ash.
Where did it end, our life-long pledge?
Three nights you came into my dreams.
The flowing water is gone forever;   5
Will the floating cloud be detained?
Sitting, I watch the emerging morning sun;
Birds are flying about in pairs.

(*YSCCC* 9/107–108)

The dream described in the second poem is the most puzzling of the three. We know from references elsewhere that Yüan Chen's wife died in the fall of 809 while he was conducting an inspection tour in Tung-ch'uan. When she was buried three months later at the ancestral cemetery in Hsien-yang, he was unable to attend the burial.[48] In this poem, however, he uses the ancient ancestral burial ground as the setting for the dream. The "jade flower" symbolizes Ch'eng-chih, whose other given name, Hui-ts'ung, means "orchid." In a sense, the ancient burial ground in its waste and desolation may represent the poet's life without her, or his present mood. What puzzles me is the reference to the distant village for which the poet holds hope. Does it project a subconscious wish for a change, a repudiation of his own morbid grief, or a hope for remarriage?

The third poem, like the first, is again addressed to his wife. He mentions that she has come to him in a dream for three nights; he does not, however, give the particulars of the third dream. What is of special interest in the third poem is that the poet seems to have come to a complete realization of the irrevocable finality of the division between life and death, and to understand the mutability of life, which is compared to flowing water, passing and gone forever.[49] Despite the imagery of his heart being like dead ashes in the early part of the poem, the concluding couplet clearly introduces a new hope, symbolized by the emerging morning sun. The "birds flying in pairs" contrasts with and accentuates his present loneliness; it may also, at the same time, project the wishful thinking of Yüan Chen for a new marriage, which, in fact, took place about 815. His new wife, P'ei Shu, courtesy name Jou-chih, was mentioned in one of his poems sent to Po Chü-i that autumn.

If I may be allowed to speculate further, the third dream that is not described in "Three Dreams in Chiang-ling" could very well be the subject of the following poem.[50]

[Poem 61]

Dreaming of A Well[51]

> I dreamt I climbed to a high plateau
> Where there was a well.
> I climbed high, wishing to quench my thirst

In the eagerly sought cool, deep pool.
Going around the well, I looked down   5
And saw myself reflected inside.
Floating on the water was a pitcher that had fallen,
But there was no rope on the well-head to draw it out.
For fear the pitcher would soon sink,
I ran in search of help.   10
I ran through the village on the plateau;
The village was deserted but the dogs were fierce.
I ran back alone and went around the well,
My loud weeping choked with sobs.
The sobbing roused me out of my dream,   15
And I awoke in a silent room;
The lamp flickered its green flame,
In the light my tears glittered like crystals,
The bell sounded its midnight chime.
Too restless to sleep, I tried to collect my wits;   20
Suddenly I remembered the burial ground of Hsien-yang
With its thousand acres of wilderness.
The ground was thick, the graves were deep,
And the dead were interred in the dark pits.
The pits were too deep to vault,   25
Yet the spirits of the dead could transcend all.
Tonight she who dwells in the Yellow Springs
Has transformed into a pitcher to renew our pledge.
Thinking of this my eyes are flooded with tears,
And the flooding tears drench my lapel.   30
Only in a state between waking and dreaming
Do I sense the real loss between life and death.

The time will come when we can share the same grave,
But what if my life goes on too long?
And what if our ghosts, one old one new   35
Will not recognize each other when they meet?
Endless doubts in my mind whirl round and round
As I sit watching the sky turning bright.
I chant aloud my dream of the well
In the morning splendor of spring.   40

                                        (*YSCCC* 9/106–107)

   This poem is fascinating, because the poetic imagery, while
coherent in itself, is replete with symbolism. Here the poet does
not see his wife, as in the first section of "Three Dreams in

Chiang-ling"; nor does he see her grave, as in the second section of that series. Instead, he dreams of the pitcher and the well into which it sank. One need not resort to Freudian or Jungian psychology to understand these dream symbols. Both the pitcher and water are recognizable *yin* or female symbols in the Chinese tradition. The high plateau, on the other hand, is the *yang* or male symbol. The sexual connotation of the poet's longing and desire for the water to quench his thirst is only too apparent to need elucidation. What is intriguing is that the poet, lacking our knowledge of modern psychology, could give us a plausible dream interpretation connecting the pitcher of his dream to his wife's spirit and the well to the Yellow Springs or the shades, which is the ultimate *yin*.

The last dream Yüan Chen had of Ch'eng-chih came five or six years after her death. Yüan Chen had returned to Ch'ang-an at the end of 814 after serving at Chiang-ling since 810 and was on his way south to T'ung-chou in Szechwan. It was most probable that he had just been married to his second wife, P'ei Jou-chih, in the capital before setting out for his new post.

[Poem 62]

Dreaming of Ch'eng-chih

The candle was out, the boat wind-tossed—suddenly I awoke
    from my dream
In which you asked me repeatedly about my sailing south.
Sleepless, I sat till dawn without a word;
All night long pounded the waves of Tung-t'ing Lake.
                  (*YSCCC* 9/111)

These lyrics by Yüan Chen about his wife are indeed moving. But those written closer to his wife's death are charged with even greater emotional intensity. Memories of the past contrast sharply with his present state of mind. The following poems convey the poet's various moods in bereavement.

[Poem 63]

Sobering Up[52]

Once in Chi-shan ward I became drunk;
Amid laughter the maids of Lord Hsieh helped me to my feet.

Tonight I became intoxicated as before,
But when I awoke there was only the sound of weeping.
$$(YSCCC \quad 9/102)$$

[Poem 64]
                    Grief in a Lonely Night
—To Secretary Chang, who had also recently lost his wife.

 The last spark in the fire is gone,
 The dim lamp casts light from an inch of flame.
 Cold wind through the bamboo smites my face;
 Hard snow drops from the eaves to the front steps.
 The cries of a lone crane string across the sky;   5
 Its chicks shudder through the chills of night.
 There could only be Secretary Chang
 To understand my present mood.
$$(YSCCC \quad 9/109)$$

[Poem 65]
                    The Empty House[53]
[Author's note:] "On the night of the fourteenth of the tenth month"

 At dawn I leave the empty house
 And ride to the empty censor's office.
 I fill the day with trifling affairs
 And return alone to an empty house.
 Moonlight pierces through dark crevices,   5
 The burnt-out wick drops its remaining ash.
 My heart goes to Hsien-yang road
 On which her hearse passed last night.
$$(YSCCC \quad 9/103)$$

[Poem 66]
                    Bamboo Mat

 The bamboo mat covering the mattress—
 I cannot bear to roll it up.
 It reminds me of the time when she first came
 And I watched her spread it out.
$$(YSCCC \quad 9/105)$$

[Poem 67]
                Spreading the Old Mosquito Net

 Between life and death the years have stretched,
 A thousand miles I have crossed from north to south.

Even at home I can never see you again,
How much less are the chances in a strange land?

The clothes you sewed for me are threadbare, 5
And I forgot to bring the letters you wrote.
Only this fine gauze mosquito net
Has traveled with me far and near.

It used to spread above our matrimonial bed,
Covering the wings of the mandarin ducks. 10
Alas, now one half of it covers emptiness,
Though its former color remains unfaded.
After pacing to and fro I am ready for bed
But how can I quiet my emotional turmoil?
Sweet were those happy hours of the past; 15
A void now fills my sad, lone soul.

Through the cracks shines the slanting moon,
In the pale light the empty bed is dark.
To console myself I try to be rational,
But I weep in my dreams for old memories. 20
You shared my life of poverty, with little to enjoy.
Cut down in your prime, your vain efforts are remembered.
Who knows how much time there is left for me,
Why must I hasten myself to the end?
The moth dances in the candle flame, 25
The silkworm weaves on the tree branches;
Their destruction is self-inflicted,
Others are powerless to prevent it.
Most partings are due to chance meetings.
Evil influences must be put to a stop. 30
What is past should not be relived,
In a future life we may rejoice at having already met.

(*YSCCC* 9/108–109)

The most famous of all of Yüan Chen's poems, those which are
anthologized in the famous *Three Hundred Poems of T'ang*,[54] are
the "Three Elegies." These three poems are frequently grouped
together, but they were not necessarily composed at the same
time.[55] All speak with deep-felt emotion of the life of hardship
and poverty his wife had shared with him in their early days of
marriage, and his inability to make it up to her now that his

circumstances have improved. The impact of these poems is
all the more powerful because of their transparent sincerity
of tone and simplicity of utterance. Indeed, very few elegiac
poems throughout the history of Chinese literature can rival
these three poems of Yüan Chen.

[Poem 68]
Three Elegies[56]
I

The youngest daughter of Lord Hsieh, his favorite child,
After marrying Ch'ien-lou, her lifestyle changed.
Seeing I needed clothes, she searched for her wicker basket;
For me to buy wine, she gave up her gold hairpin.
With wild herbs for table fare, we enjoyed the long beanstalks.   5
Fallen leaves for fuel, we gazed at the ancient locust tree.
Today my salary exceeds a hundred thousand cash,
All I can do is pour libation and offer sacrifice.

[Poem 69]
II

In the past we joked about death coming between us,
Suddenly it has come to pass in front of my eyes.
Almost all of your dresses have now been given away,
Only your needlework stays, as I can't bear to part with it.
Recalling your old sentiments, I am more kind to our maids
    and valets;   5
Because of my dreams of you, I make offerings of alms.
Well I know this sorrow is common to all mankind,
But few have known poverty together as did we.

[Poem 70]
III

Sitting alone I mourn for you and for myself:
How much time is left in my life's span?
With no male heir, like Teng Yu I must bow to my fate;
In vain the elegies of P'an Yüeh fail to soothe my grief.
What can I hope for but to share the gloom of your tomb?   5
There is little chance that we will meet again in another life.
But I shall keep my eyes open through the long night,
To compensate for the knitted brows in your burdened life with me.
                         (YSCCC 9/104)

The following poem is especially touching because of the element of realism—shown here are Ch'eng-chih's simplistic nature and childish faith in superstitious practices. Judging by Yüan Chen's own aversion or objection to such superstitions as crow-worship and shamanism, the poem is especially significant as an indication of the poet's growing maturity and tolerance, and the realization that nothing matters in life except "the quality of affection."[57] The act of her crow-worship matters little but her love and concern for him are forever remembered.

[Poem 71]

> Listening to Yü Chi-chih Playing the Tune of "The Crow
> Caws at Night" on the Lute[58]

While you play the prelude of "The Crow Caws at Night,"
I compose this *yüeh-fu* verse to relate an ancient story:
Once there lived a young wife
Whose husband was imprisoned;
Before the official pardon came,   5
A crow reported the news to the wife.
In tears she prostrated herself in front of the crow,
Who cawed sadly as the wife offered her prayers.
Someone later composed the tune of the "Cawing Crow."
So moving is the *Wu* tune on the mournful strings.   10

Four or five years ago, when I was an imperial censor,
My proposals to the throne offended the chief minister.
Disgraced, I suffered imprisonment and demotion,
And banishment away from home.
When I was reunited with my wife, she wept pearls of tears   15
And confessed to me that she, too, worshipped the crow at night;
"Your return was due to the efficacy of the crow";
And she decorated the crow's plate and called the sorceress.

Now you have played this tune for me many times,
The sorrowful notes always reduce me to tears;   20
Your music touches me to the quick in a special way:
Yesterday the crow cawed and the *t'ung* leaves fell,
But she who worshipped the crow for my sake,
Has been buried in a Hsien-yang grave.
                                            (*YSCCC* 9/1056)

Besides these elegiac poems for his wife, Yüan Chen also wrote poems mourning the death of his children, some of whom died in infancy, some at a tender age. Two female children were addressed by name: for Chiang-chen there is one poem; for Fan-tzu, two (one of which is eighty lines in length). There are ten short poems mourning a son named Ching, who must have been born to his second wife, née P'ei, and who died when he was nine years old. "Mourning My Son" consists of ten quatrains, with a note by the author ascribing their composition to the period when the poet was in the *Han-lin* Academy (821–822).

[Poem 72]

Mourning My Son[59]
(Ten Verses)

Satirized with "Pelican," I could see my fault;
The misfortune brought by a horse was an injustice to you.
Alone in the courtyard, I lean idly against a tree,
The clamorous cicadas screech toward evening.

You could just barely distinguish east from west,   5
But knew nothing about law and authority;
Never having tasted independence in your life,
Whom can you rely on during your journey to Hades?

Your mother, drowned in sorrow, cries night after night,
I, being busy, can only mourn from time to time,   10
Before I cease grieving, light stirs in the east—
'Tis the hour you were ready for school.

I forbade you to eat too many pears and nuts
        for fear you would get sick;
Eager to prepare you for school,
        I tried to teach you poetry and history;
To guide you I employed the rod more than love—   15
For that I cry three times over in remorse.

May you be reborn in the Supreme Lotus, the realm of truth,
But *Tushita* is far away from the ways of this world.
Our *karma* differs: many obstacles in our separate paths,
I do not know if in the future life we shall meet again.   20

I grieve that you had no brothers,
And pity myself for having no male heir.
The desolate edifice of a lecture hall is still there,
Yet whose horses or carriages will pass through its gate?

In the past my sideburns were like those of P'an Yüeh,   25
In my declining years I share the experience of Teng Yu.
Amid all my woes there is one consoling thought:
No longer need I worry for my offspring.

Long years of bitter circumstances brought no end of woe,
For you alone, son, must I lose my wits?   30
For your mother's sake I try to dispel my grief—
In the depth of night the chants of sutras mingle with my tears.

The crow hatched eight eggs: seven are lost;
The gibbon cries three times at the lone moon.
In the silent empty chamber at dawn,   35
Brushing the curtains, a pair of swallows lead their young.

Frequently young birds fall into the flowing river,
Each night the parent birds wait by their old nest;
If such sorrow does not tear their hearts to shreds,
Their mourning cries will increase with the years.   40

(*YSCCC* 9/113–114)

III *Poems of Miscellaneous Moods*

From the poems cited above, one can readily see that poetry
was part and parcel of Yüan Chen's life. He wrote poetry for
public circulation, for self-indulgence, or for entertainment; and
he wrote to instruct, to remonstrate, to protest, to satirize, to
vindicate, to console, to confess, and to mourn. Some of his
poems fall neatly into thematic arrangement, as I have shown.
But there are others in which the theme seems to be less
significant than the mood they depict or convey. And Yüan
Chen can truly be said to be a poet of many moods. Even among
those elegiac poems that are charged with emotional intensity
one can detect a wide spectrum of varying moods, from a desire
for death, utter loneliness, and desolation to vague regret, wist-
fulness, and anticipation. Indeed, his was a highly complex
personality; he was a man of quick temper and changing moods.

He led a colorful and eventful life full of ups and downs;
he vacillated from high expectation to deep despair. Inevitably,
his poetry reflects all of these feelings.

In some poems, however, there is what seems to be intentional
obscurity. It is difficult to tell whether he means what he says,
or whether he is being sarcastic, saying the opposite of what he
feels. "The Music of Homesickness," for instance, is one example
of such a poem.

[Poem 73]

The Music of Homesickness[60]

In the mountains, the music that provokes my homesickness
Comes from the chirpings of "homesick birds."
"But you birds are native to these mountains,
Why are you known by such a name?"
It was said that these mountain roads   5
Were taken by travelers driven from their homes,
And their dark sorrow so filled the air
That it caused these birds to be born.

Although I have left my native soil,
I harbor no homeless grief.   10
Both grief and joy stem from the heart;
Neither honor nor disgrace would disturb me.
In this floating life I would be glad
To lay my head on a plot eight feet by ten.
Personal safety is my contentment,   15
Why should I rejoice to be only in the capital?
Life is the root of all *Tao*
And death is heaven's way for balance;
Why ask how far or how near is my destination?
What matters if I die untimely or live to P'eng-tzu's age?   20

Look at octogenarian Chao, the minister of labor,
Who is still nimble of limbs at his age,
He spent twenty years in Chiao-chou,
Before returning to Ch'ang-an.
Shortly after his arrival at the capital   25
He was sent back to Chiao-chou,
Then he was transferred to Chiang-ling.
At last he was recalled to court,

After the accession of the new emperor.
Now he is an active high-ranking minister;   30
No sign of malaria shows on his skin,
Hale and hardy, he has a healthy appetite.
Yet man's life is as brief as day and night,
Death is fast like falling stars,
And hearses exit by the four city gates   35
Whether fever or malaria is the cause.

I am barely over thirty,
Not yet half of my life's span.
The journey to Chiang-ling is rather short
And the Ch'u state is familiar and its water is pure.   40
I have longed to visit the Temple of Jade Springs;
And am anxious to climb its towers.
This exile will enrich me with experience,
For I will have time to appreciate everything.
Ruddy coarse grain will fill my stomach;   45
Green spring water will quench my thirst.
My door will be open to all guests;
I will send letters to comfort my brothers.
At leisure I'll work to perfect my rhymes.
When bored I'll read the nine classics.   50
Beyond my personal needs I seek nothing,
I let the present take its natural course.
This resolution I made long ago;
Who cares to go after fame and glory?
So I do not mind my low office,   55
In court or out in the field, power crumbles.
Is it not easy to submit one's heart
And leave the treacherous to God's punishment?
All created things have their true nature,
How much more is man the superior being?   60

Gold, even buried, will not tarnish from dirt;
Jade, when it falls, does not sound like tile;
A broken sword remains sharp even in inches;
The shattered mirror is bright in every fragment.

I may be captured by the enemy;   65
I may be used as an instrument.
But my heart will never die—
Its sincerity penetrates gold and stone.

If only sincerity is at its utmost
The *Tao* will prevail, no matter what the adversity.   70
How trivial are the birds in these mountains;
Their squawking is not worth my listening.
(YSCCC 1/1–2)

The original title for "The Music of Homesickness" has two
possible readings: *Szu-kuei yüeh* (literally: think, return home,
music); or *Szu-kuei lo* (literally: think, return, happiness). The
ambiguity lies in the third character, for which both readings
are possible. I have chosen the first reading, because of the
reference to the songs of birds, which is also called *szu-kuei*
(i.e., the cuckoo birds whose songs bring homesickness to distant wanderers). Although no date of composition is given,
there is reference in the poem to the poet's being thirty-one
(thirty-two, by Chinese calculation) years old, which would
place the poem in 810, when he was on his way to Chiang-ling.
If the banishment was painful to him, he seemed to try to see
the brighter side of a dim future or to reconcile himself to his
fate.

"Dispelling Illness" was written in 815, after he was transferred to Szechwan, where he contracted malaria. He could have
been close to death, as indicated by another poem. Yet the
mood evoked here is not despondent; it is one ultimately of
acceptance and faith in the immortality of man. Self-pity is encountered in some of his poems, but here his main concern
seems to be to console others over his impending death, to
comfort his loved ones.

[Poem 74]

Dispelling Illness[61]

Since time immemorial men have been unable to escape death;
Their names are no longer remembered.
This year, in the capital alone,
Death has swept away both young and old;
Secretary Yü had barely reached forty,   5
On the threshold of a glorious career;
Censor Li was in his thirty-ninth year,
His clear voice still lingers in the imperial court;
Then there was Chao Ch'ang the octogenarian

Who won three victories by his prowess.   10
In life they walked separate paths,
Now they are denizens of the same place of shades.
Their mourning families share a common grief
For their loved one's mortal fate.
Perfect equity is reached in the end;   15
Be it an ageless tortoise or the ephemeral mushroom,
Death deals fairly with all between heaven and earth.

Being stricken with illness in this region
I could care less.
Even if I die this very moment   20
My existence would have been complete.
Supposing I could live to be a hundred
I do not know what more I could have done.
Besides, I have learned the Buddhist way:
To consider this body no more than an abode.   25
In moving from one room to another,
Is there to be any entanglement?
My former existences are but past imprints,
The future life lies ahead.
Weary only of the ceaseless journey of life,   30
Need I fear that there is no path to follow?

A dragon shedding its scales does not die,
The cicada still sings after molting;
Should it not be the same when the soul leaves the body?
Why is man mystified by this natural process?   35
To my dear friends and brothers
I send these lines of consolation,
So that they may find comfort in my fate
And ignore the prattle of the world.

(*YSCCC* 7/82–83)

A series of five poems under the title "Wild Words" exemplifies
a different, even more expansive mood.

[Poem 75]
Wild Words[62]
(In five verses)

I
Lately, whenever I drink, I sing out loud.
Being drunk, I dance; my words sound wild.

Five magnums of wine can't quench my thirst;
Ten more rounds of flowing cups are still not enough.
I brush aside the enemy in front of my eyes,   5
And for rank and fortune, I don't give a damn.
Death to me is ultimate liberation; life, too, I can muddle
    through.
Is anyone capable of hurting me?

II

Should I hold a secret grudge against Ch'ang-sha?
The cloud is at home wherever it roams.
Coarse wine and unpolished rice satisfy me as they did the
    Fisherman;
I receive my meal with open mouth like the heavenly crow.
Awaiting the phoenix, a thousand stems of bamboo shoot
    upward;   5
Bending with the wind, the willows swing to one direction.
Providence provides plenty of rain and dew
For me to thrive and sustain my life.

III

Lightning flashes and thunder rolls on;
How can they threaten a madman who fears no death?
If I were burned to a cinder by the thunderclap,
Rather than having my bones buried, I'd rather their ashes be
    scattered to the wind—
Perchance they become butterflies resting on flowering trees,   5
Or change into river fish with scales of brocade.
O you wicked dragon, wherever you are,
How can you destroy me who is one with Nature?

IV

Since my heart can be at peace everywhere,
Why waste my days gazing at tree-clad peaks?
The jade flower remains cool even by the fire,
The lily pads are dry while still in water.
Ning Ch'i tending the cow was only a fairy tale;   5
Lu T'ung singing of the phoenix was also nonsense.
Sun Teng was silent, Ch'i-ch'i was content:
Each to his own happiness by following his instinct.

V

For thirty years I have walked on this earth,
I traveled far, I acquired a passing fame.

Twice banished, I ought to know my lot.
Several times I stood in the imperial court; where is that
    glory now?
I only seek my cup to be covered by pine needles;   5
Sheltered, I let the willow branches grow by my elbows.
When I die I would like to be buried near a kiln
And be made into wine jugs for others to use.

                         (*YSCCC* 18/221–22)

The hyperbolic, boastful mood expressed in these poems is rather rare in his poetry. One might perhaps attribute his lack of restraint to the influence of drinking, as he himself suggests in the first verse. However, one can hardly consider Yüan Chen to have been a heavy drinker as one would many other Chinese poets. Even though he occasionally praised the joys of wine, his verse on drinking rarely achieves the sense of uninhibited abandon encountered, for instance, in the poetry of Li Po. Among his poems on this subject, there are ten poems of varying length written in the ancient style (i.e., with uneven meters and line lengths) under the composite title "Have a Drink" (*Yu Chiu*). The last, the shortest of the group, which is included here in full, is more political than convivial.

[Poem 76]

                  Have a Drink

Have a drink, have a drink, and I'll offer another toast.
I offer a toast to my heart, for whatever it may aspire:
That peace be in heaven and peace be on earth;
That people be in good health and ripe in their years;
That the phoenix may soar, followed by mandarin ducks;   5
That the dragon may prevail, pursued by a thoroughbred;
That the sun may shine stronger than stars.
I wish to nourish the orchids and be rid of poisonous weeds.
I wish that heaven would grant men's wishes.
But should heaven fail to grant my wishes,   10
I'll drink another cup to fulfill myself.

                         (*YSCCC* 75/325)

Such drinking songs, however, have little to do with the pleasure of drinking or the effects of wine. More expressive of

Yüan Chen's drinking moods are perhaps the shorter pieces, such as these:

[Poem 77]
Drinking Alone

A tree of fragrance, it must be spring!
Riding in a carriage, I am clad with dust.
The peach blossoms share my jokes; the oriole speaks.
I drink alone and sleep alone—who cares where I am.
(*YSCCC* 16/197)

[Poem 78]
Drunk First

Today, facing the wine cup, I am a disgrace:
Before the third toast, I can pour no more.
I wonder why, beneath the blossoms, I am always drunk first—
Partly because the spring wind has abetted my intoxication.
(*YSCCC* 16/197)

[Poem 79]
Cold

The malarial weather by the river was warm;
By the first part of last month the flowering plum had
    already faded.
Last night the north wind suddenly arrived;
I am happy to find today turning cold.
A sheet of ice forms on the shallow pond,   5
And snow heaps against the bamboo fence.
I have just filled another cup of warm wine,
But who is there to enjoy it with me?
Drinking alone only increases one's loneliness.
(*YSCCC* 7/82)

The dominant mood in these poems is loneliness. Despite the close friendship formed with several kindred souls, Yüan Chen spent more than half of his life away from the capital and separated from his dear ones. To compensate for the resulting lack of human companionship, he looked to nature for consolation. The oriole mentioned in "Drinking Alone" and the poem

that follows recall the heroine's name in *"Hui-chen chi,"* but
it is entirely possible that in both cases the oriole is simply one
of the creatures of the wild that has captured his interest.

[Poem 80]

Wandering Alone[63]

> In this remote region
> One hardly meets a kindred soul.
> To climb the mountain, I follow the crane;
> Sipping my wine, I await the oriole.
> The flowers replace Hsi Shih's face;
> The fountains here are purer than Wei Chieh.
> The noisy pelicans cover the wilderness in spring,
> And there is no end to their monotones.
>
> (*YSCCC* 15/180)

The proverbial beauty of Hsi Shih (fifth century B.C.) and
the perfect appearance of Wei Chieh (286–312 A.D.) are less to
be admired than the beauty and purity of nature. Yet nature per
se seldom engages Yüan Chen's undivided attention. One can
fully appreciate nature only when emptied of a desire for
name and fame. Does the following poem, "Living in Retirement," reflect, then, the true sentiments of the poet, or does it
simply represent a passing mood during one of his imposed
retirements?

[Poem 81]

Living in Retirement

> A rustic, I love to live in seclusion.
> Nearby are tall pines; in the distance, mountains.
> All day long I watch the clouds, my heart unattached;
> Often I look at the moon in the leisure of the night.
> My world is in the teapot and beyond the universe,   5
> Name and fame are dreams between dusk and dawn.
> Across the vast sea, I think of the thousand year old crane
> Who, temporarily detained in the city, will return.
>
> (*YSCCC* 16/195)

The image of the crane, like that of the oriole, appears often
in Yüan Chen's poems. But the crane inhabits the poem more

for its traditional symbolic meaning—freedom and detachment from worldly cares—than as an object of natural beauty. In the following poem, Yüan Chen compares himself and his close friends to the crane, which can not get along with the "startling crow and squawking sparrow," and is not likely to return to the maddening crowd.

[Poem 82]
    Harmonizing Secretary P'ei's Poem, "The Crane's Flight"

  Crane, crane, whither do you fly?
  Can you long endure the startling crow and squawking sparrow?
  The river is so clear that the bottom shows;
  The thatched hut is here still,
  But that spark of white light will never return.   5
                         (YSCCC 16/92)

    Fundamentally oriented toward the human world, Yüan Chen has never been considered a poet of nature, even though nature imagery abounds in his poetry. More often than not, descriptions of nature and the use of nature imagery are subsidiary to the main theme. They are used to elicit a mood or to provide frames of reference for philosophical speculation, or as symbols of political allegory. Among his nature images, Yüan Chen seems to have had a special interest in flowers. In his poems, flowers appear more frequently than mountains and rivers. A number of his poems are either about or addressed to flowering plants and trees. In "Fallen Blossoms Over the River," the blossoms are treated in a rather conventional way: as a "pathetic fallacy," they reflect the sad mood of the poet sailing on the river during one of his exiles from home. Nostalgia for his native soil, or the pain of deracination, is depicted more explicitly in the two poems entitled "Transplanting Flowers."

[Poem 83]
                Fallen Blossoms Over the River[64]

    Sunset simmers on the eastward current of Chia-ling River;
    Myriad pear blossoms pursue the river wind.
    The most heart-rending moment—
    When the petals are half in the water, half in the air.
                        (YSCCC 17/212–13)

[Poem 84]

Transplanting Flowers

I

I brought along a couple of mountain flowers;
They began to wilt without their native soil.
If you wish to know how a northerner fared in the south,
Just look at these southern flowers being brought to the north.

II

Southern flowers, moved to the north, can hardly survive:
All day long I watch them in my boat.
Even if they die before my eyes,
It is better than abandoning them by a deserted fence.

(*YSCCC* 19/235)

There is an identification of the flowers with the poet. Little descriptive attention is accorded the flowers he has transplanted. They are simply referred to as mountain flowers from the south, and it seems that the poet is more interested in his own condition than in the condition of the flowers.

One flower that received full and detailed treatment from Yüan Chen is the mountain loquat. In a fairly long poem by that title, the beauty of its blossom is meticulously described and even personified. In the concluding stanza, however, the poet is identified with the flower—both possess a secret fragrance but are neglected and unappreciated.

[Poem 85]

Mountain Loquats[65]

The mountain loquats—
Their flowers are like peonies splashing blood.
One year I rode by Green Hill on the pony express
In the season when the mountain was covered with their blossoms;
The loquat boughs were heavy-laden with blooming beauties.   5
The fragrant buds shaded by the leaves were only half open—
As if holding their red sleeves to support their chins,
The knots of their vermillion purse were slowly loosened,
To show a profusion of golden threads—the stamens,
The twisting, turning intricacies of the coral cluster.   10
In the breeze the petals whirled about like flying skirts;
Against the sunlight their brightness hurt the eyes.
Leaning toward the water, bending halfway down from the cliffs,

Wrapped in clouds, mist-concealed, they seemed most melancholic:
Lu Chu [on the tower] silently hurled herself down;   15
Emperor Wu's eyes pierced the sky for the vanished soul.
Beautiful shapes and colors are universally admired,
But I am partial to shy and melancholy charms.
When I try to tell others, no one understands;
I can only impart this to Lo-t'ien.   20
When I came to Ku-k'ou, I first inquired about these flowers,
But by the time I arrived at the mountains, they had faded.
Exiled to T'ung-chou, I was late by ten days;
And I could not feast on their blossoms for another year.
Mountain loquats!   25
Why are you so foolish as to remain in the mountains?
The skies ten thousand *li* above cannot be seen clearly;
No sound can reach the emperor in the Ninth Heaven;
The apricots in the garden may intoxicate people,
The willow branches near the road may be broken by young men.   30
Because of your secret fragrance comparable to the ancient sages,
I would sit in the cold of Fan-hsi and let the officials groan.
(*YSCCC* 26/328–29)

The most frequently quoted of Yüan Chen's poems on flowers
is probably "The Chrysanthemums." The poem holds a special
charm because of its pristine simplicity of expression.

[Poem 86]
The Chrysanthemums[66]

Clusters of autumn blossoms encircle my house
    as if it were the home of T'ao;
Everywhere along the fence, they glow in the slanting sun.
It is not that I am partial to chrysanthemums of all flowers,
But when they are gone there will be no more blossoms.
(*YSCCC* 16/194)

It is not likely that Yüan Chen implied an identification between himself and the great poet of nature, T'ao Ch'ien, or that
he compared himself or his poetry to the chrysanthemums, which
are symbols of endurance. It is possible, however, to see that
Yüan Chen was aware of the long literary tradition that preceded him, and that he hoped that his poetry might have the
quality symbolized by the chrysanthemum.

Yüan Chen's spirit of innovation and experimentation is also manifested in the physical structure of his poetry. Some of his poems categorized as *yüeh-fu* do not so much conform to the *yüeh-fu* tradition as they adopt the freedom exercised in *yüeh-fu* composition. Moreover, he also experimented with certain poetic structures that no one before him had ever attempted. In a short poem entitled "Tea," Yüan Chen attempted to create a physical poetic structure that is akin to what we would term concrete poetry. The poem cannot be considered a serious poem containing significant ideas, but it is one of a kind and unique in its physical pattern. The poem is composed of fifty-five Chinese characters, which may be arranged into thirteen lines in the shape of a triangle. Except for the first line, which consists of one word, "tea (*ch'a*)" which is both the topic and the rhyme word, the twelve remaining lines are couplets ranging from two to seven characters in length. Since each Chinese character occupies an equal portion of space, I use Xs to illustrate the visual pattern of the poem, which seems to resemble the tea plant. The original poem, however, was written in the traditional manner with one character following another without a break; separations of lines are distinguishable only through end rhymes.

```
                  X
               X     X
               X     X
            X     X     X
            X     X     X
         X     X     X     X
         X     X     X     X
      X     X     X     X     X
      X     X     X     X     X
   X     X     X     X     X     X
   X     X     X     X     X     X
X     X     X     X     X     X     X
X     X     X     X     X     X     X
```

[Poem 87]

Tea

Fragrant   tea
Tender leaves
Appreciated by all poets
A treasure to Buddhists   5
Ground with sculptured white jade
Filtered through crimson silk gauze
Well-brewed, it shows the color of yellow pollen
Poured out, it shimmers in the cup like pure gold
I savor its flavor often in the company of the full moon   10
At early dawn I drink it always before the morning cloud
It cleanses past and present worries from those who are weary
Knowing that I will be intoxicated, how can I sing of its praise
(*CTShih* 423/4652)

CHAPTER 6

The Author of Prose Fiction

I F one has been impressed with the versatility exhibited by
Yüan Chen in his poetry, especially in his attention to detail
in the narrative poems, then it may not be surprising to find
that he was also an impressive writer of fiction, even though
only one extant piece of T'ang prose fiction is attributed to him.
While his fame as a poet seems to have declined shortly after
his death, Yüan Chen's prose fiction, on the other hand, grew in
popularity and continued to exercise its influence on Chinese
literature.

The beginnings of Chinese fiction go back long before Yüan
Chen's time. However, pre-T'ang fiction is for the most part
rudimentary in development, limited in scope, and often crude
in style. Most pre-T'ang narratives take the form of anecdotes,
fables, fairy tales, and supernatural stories that heavily betray
Taoist and Buddhist influences. It was not until the ninth century that a new narrative genre known as the *ch'uan-ch'i*
("transmitting the marvelous") evolved.[1] In this newly developed
prose genre, greater attention was paid to structure and style.
The *ku-wen* movement, which promoted a simple and elegant
literary style of writing, must have stimulated the rapid growth
of this form of prose fiction, which in turn helped to bring about
the success of the *ku-wen* movement. Although the traditional-
minded scholars continued to look down upon fiction as a
frivolous, subliterary form, mainly for entertainment and unworthy of serious attention, many scholars, however, enjoyed
reading and writing prose fiction in private. As a matter of fact,
it had become a common practice for candidates of the literary
examinations to submit writings of this kind to their sponsors
and examiners prior to the examinations as proof of their literary
qualifications. This practice came to be known as *wen-chüan*
("warming-up writings"). For the freedom allowed by this

literary genre afforded the author an opportunity to exhibit his versatility and creativity. Yüan Chen's famous prose fiction, "The Story of Ying-ying,"[2] could very well be the product of such practice. For it is believed to have been in circulation around the time he took the palace examination in 804.

"The Story of Ying-ying" is preserved in the *T'ai-p'ing Miscellany* (*T'ai-p'ing kuang-chi*), a stupendous collection of miscellaneous writings of the past compiled by Li Fang (925–996) in the Sung dynasty. This popular title, derived from the name of the heroine of the story, which was known by the original title, "*Hui-chen chi*" ("Meeting with an Immortal"), derived from "*Hui-chen shih*," a poem of sixty lines, which was admittedly written by Yüan Chen, the narrator (who makes his appearance in the story as the male protagonist's friend), and which keynotes the narrative. The change of the title could be taken as an indication of public interest shifting its focus from the male to the female protagonist in the story.

Although by no means the only prose romance written in the *ch'uan-ch'i* genre, Yüan Chen's "Story of Ying-ying" is by general agreement one of the finest examples of its kind. In fact, it so captured the public imagination that in later centuries the story was retold in many forms, frequently in verse and drama. Among Yüan Chen's contemporaries, Li Shen and Yang Chü-yüan both were inspired to write poems commenting on this ill-fated romance. A century or so later, Chao Shih-lin (fl. tenth century) composed a ballad in twelve stanzas retelling the same love story. Among the various poetic versions of the story, the most famous is Tung Chieh-yüan's (fl. 1190–1220)[3] long narrative poem in eight *chüan* and over fifty thousand characters. Written in the *chu-kung-tiao* (music medley) genre and under the title "Ts'ui Ying-ying Waiting for the Moon in the Western Chamber," the originally tragic romance of Yüan Chen was given a happy ending. Tung's work served as the blueprint for a full-fledged play (in twenty acts) by Wang Shih-fu (fl. thirteenth century) under the title *Romance of the Western Chamber* (*Hsi-hsiang chi*). More adaptations of the play were made in subsequent centuries, some as recent as the late nineteenth century; for the love story has continued to intrigue poets and playwrights and audiences even to this day.

Since several English versions of "The Story of Ying-ying" are readily available,[4] I will not give the story in full here. Occasional excerpts and a synopsis should prove sufficient for the purposes of discussion. Briefly, the story unfolds as follows.

A young scholar surnamed Chang, on his way to the capital to compete in the metropolitan examination, takes up lodging in a monastery near Pu-chou to prepare himself for the upcoming task. By coincidence, a certain widow, Mrs. Ts'ui, née Cheng, returning home with her two children from an outlying post upon the death of her husband, happens to be temporarily residing in the same monastery, which, in accordance with the custom of the day, provides spacious quarters for guests and patrons. By further coincidence, a band of soldiers in the vicinity has mutinied and turned to banditry after the death of its commander. With the monastery threatened by the outlaws, Mrs. Ts'ui is extremely fearful for the safety of her family. Chang, through his connections with a general stationed in Pu-chou, sends for help and averts imminent danger to all. In gratitude, Mrs. Ts'ui invites Chang to dinner and to meet her family. In the course of their conversation, Chang discovers that his mother, also née Cheng, and Mrs. Ts'ui are distant cousins. Mrs. Ts'ui urges her teenage daughter, Ying-ying, to come out to greet Chang as an elder brother. She does so with great reluctance. Chang is smitten at once by her extraordinary beauty. He solicits help from Ying-ying's maid, Hung-niang, to be a go-between, through whom he sends two love poems titled "Spring Songs" (these poems are mentioned, but no texts are given in the story). Ying-ying responds with the following poem entitled "Bright Moon on the Fifteenth Day":

> I wait for the moon in the western chamber;
> The door is ajar to welcome the breeze.
> When the flower shadows stir against the wall,
> I fancy that a precious person has come.

Chang interprets the poem to be an open invitation for a rendezvous on a designated date, the fifteenth of the month, when the moon is at its fullest. Since he receives the poem on the fourteenth of the second month, he waits impatiently for the night to fall on the following day, so that he can climb over the eastern wall, using a tree as a ladder. When at last he reaches the western chamber for the tryst, the door is actually half open. But when he enters the room, he finds only the maid there fast asleep. Aroused from her sleep, the startled maid asks the reason for Chang's rude intrusion. Chang claims that he is there at Ying-ying's invitation. The maid withdraws. After a long while she returns to announce that her young mistress is coming. Ying-ying finally appears, solemnly dressed and stern in expression. She rebukes Chang roundly for taking advantage of her because of her family's gratitude for his averting possible harm to them from the bandits. After her speech she retreats, leaving Chang dumbfounded and in despair.

Two weeks later, she goes to his room of her own free will and surrenders herself to him without a word of explanation. This sudden turn of events takes Chang by surprise; he is overjoyed but hardly able to believe it to be true. Even after Ying-ying leaves him, he sits in the half dawn wondering if he has just met a fair goddess in a dream. When he fails to see Ying-ying again for a fortnight, he composes a poem entitled "Meeting with an Immortal" and sends it to her.[5] After this the two meet regularly in secret in the western chamber. Finally, Chang leaves her to go to the capital to take the examination, which he fails. He writes to Ying-ying, who responds with a touching love letter full of pathos, for she has already sensed the gradual cooling of his love for her. Chang shows her letter to his friends, who are all surprised at Chang's decision to terminate the romance. The author, Yüan Chen, who presents himself in the story as an intimate friend of the protagonist, asks Chang for an explanation of his decision. Chang provides the following answer:

"Such an extraordinary creation as Ying-ying is always endowed with the power to destroy, either herself or those close to her. If she were married into wealth and influence, she might be transformed into something unimaginable. In the past, King Hsin of the Yin dynasty and King Yu of the Chou dynasty ruled great states and had thousands of chariots. Yet because of a woman, they came to a violent end, bringing destruction to their empires as well. Even today they remain objects of ridicule. My personal virtue is not so strong as to be able to withstand such devastating power as that of Miss Ts'ui. That is why I have decided to suppress my emotions and sever the relationship."[6]

That Yüan Chen was the author of the story can be attested by the fact that he admits to being the narrator when he tells us in the conclusion that he frequently related this love story at social gatherings and among friends, in order that "those who have knowledge of this will not do the same; those who have behaved in the same way will not be deluded."[7]

Another clue that points to Yüan Chen as the author is the inclusion in the story of his own poem entitled *"Hsü hui-chen shih"* ("Poem on Encountering an Immortal—A Sequel"), which is really not a sequel but more likely the poem referred to early in the narrative as having been composed by Chang, which is the exact length of Yüan Chen's poem. This romanticized, poetical description of Chang's personal experience of Ying-ying's visit duplicates and echoes clearly the first part of Yüan Chen's other romantic poem "Dream of a Spring Excursion."[8] Although in most English versions of this story Yüan Chen's poem is omitted (possibly on account of its length or tediousness, or the difficulty in rendering it into English), it has been translated by Hightower in his recent article, "Yüan Chen and 'The Story of Ying-ying.' "[9]

Stylistically, "The Story of Ying-ying" is a display of the author's narrative skill. As if to follow the rules set down by the *ku-wen* movement, the narrative is couched in concise, classical language devoid of excessive embellishment and verbosity. The entire work consists of no more than three thousand words. Yet, it contains detailed descriptions and a smooth unfolding of the dramatic situation. One special skill of the narrative art already evidenced in Yüan Chen's poetry is his attention to detail. Witness the details given in the following passage describing the scene preceding and following the consummation of their love.

A few days later, when Chang was already in bed in his quarters near the veranda, he was suddenly aroused by someone. Half awake, he was startled to see the maid Hung-niang before him, holding a pillow and a folded quilt. Touching him gently by the hand, she said, "She is coming! She is coming! Why are you sleeping?" Then she put down the bedding and disappeared. Rubbing his eyes, Chang tried to compose himself. For a long time he sat there thinking that he was still in a dream. Then he assumed a pious air and waited in dignity. Finally Ying-ying arrived, supported by her maid. She seemed to be overcome with embarrassment and looked as fragile and delicate as if she had no strength to move her limbs. Though winsome and surpassingly beautiful, she was entirely different from the somber, dignified person she had been a few days before.

It was the night of the eighteenth of the month; the slanting moon cast its glittering rays like a shower of crystal through the window and illuminated half of the bed. Chang was exultant, still imagining that an immortal being had descended upon him. After what seemed a short while the temple bell sounded, announcing the approach of dawn, and Hung-niang urged her mistress to depart. As she was led away, Ying-ying cried and groaned gently. But all night long she had never uttered a single word. Chang rose; still not quite believing that it really happened, he asked himself, "Am I dreaming?" When dawn broke, a streak of rouge was still on his arm; her perfume lingered still on his nightclothes; on the mat glittering like pearls were traces of the tears she had shed.[10]

Despite its unusual appeal and wide popularity, there is a major flaw in the work. This is the moral theme incongruously injected into the narrative, which seems to conflict with the romantic tone that runs throughout the story. By this I mean in particular the protagonist's rationalization of his decision to desert Ying-ying on moral grounds.[11] Some literary critics have argued that a philosophical or moral point is required of the *ch'uan-ch'i* genre. This is doubtful. Others who claim the fiction to be a true autobiographical account of Yüan Chen's youth regard the moralizing as a reflection of the poet's fickle personality.[12] I would like to present a third interpretation to account for some of the apparent discrepancies in the story.

If Yüan Chen was indeed the literary genius as claimed by his contemporaries, it seems rather unlikely that he would have been unaware of what seem to us to be inconsistencies in point of view. We must not rule out the possibility that these seeming incongruities were intended by the author to give the story an additional level of meaning discernible only to the attentive reader. Such an interpretation becomes even more plausible if we accept the traditional view that the story is autobiographical and that the protagonist is actually the author in disguise.[13]

One other apparent flaw in the story that corroborates this theory is in the characterization of the protagonist. Not only is Chang's character poorly delineated, but it is full of inconsistencies and contradictions. In the opening paragraph, in which Chang is first introduced, more is said of his personal integrity than of his physical appearance: "In the *chen-yüan* period (785–805 A.D.) there lived a scholar, Chang by name, who was of a gentle nature and refined manners. A man of handsome appearance, he was of strong character and personal integrity. He was opposed to anything lacking propriety."[14] The word "propriety" should be underscored, because it is a recurring term, and one which denotes the underlying motif of the entire story. Judging by the events that result from Chang's behavior, this introductory comment on Chang can be taken only as dramatic irony: "Whenever he joined his friends in social activities, he never participated in those untoward amusements that others engaged in with full enthusiasm. Occasionally he appeared to be joining the fun, but no one could make him lose his self-control. Thus he had never had any experience with the opposite sex, although he was twenty-one."[15]

Chang's sense of propriety is reiterated in his own words. When he confides to Hung-niang his love for Ying-ying and asks her to help him, he says, "From my early childhood, it has always been my nature to reject impropriety. Even on the most opportune occasions I have never made improper advances toward the fair sex . . . ."[16] Yet all of his actions show a disregard for propriety and a lack of moral principles. His behavior toward Ying-ying is outrageously improper according to Confucian ethics. Contrary to the assertion that Chang is a strong character and a man of personal integrity, he appears weak and indecisive throughout the story. His attempt to rationalize on moral grounds his desertion of Ying-ying fails to make sense, unless we are to understand that he is really a moral coward lacking in "personal virtue." The characterization of Chang is sketchy and incomplete, and the element of personal conflict between reason and passion, or the struggle between virtue and vice, assumes less meaning for Chang than it does for Ying-ying.

By contrast, Ying-ying is a more fully developed character. Her personality emerges clearly in the description of her reluctance to meet Chang at her mother's bidding. "After a long wait, Ying-ying finally entered. She was dressed casually in ordinary attire, without any fresh makeup. She seemed deeply distressed. Her locks hung loose, her dark eyebrows knit, and the rouge on her cheeks almost gone. Nevertheless, her extraordinary natural beauty was overpowering; her brilliance was bedazzling to any mortal eye. . . . She sat by her mother's side throughout the interview, with her gaze fixed and visibly depressed, as if she were on the verge of collapse."[17]

If anything, Ying-ying's contradictory behavior reflects an internal struggle, a struggle between her superego and her id. The emotional conflict within her is not stated explicitly, but is externalized in her actions and behavior. Her deep displeasure at meeting Chang initially could be attributed to her strict observance of propriety, but possibly it is because she is already aware of a temptation to fall in love with Chang and she tries to avoid it. Once she does, she does so with her eyes open and she is ready to assume the consequences—that by losing her virtue she may disqualify herself from becoming Chang's legitimate wife. This is why she never urges him to marry her, nor threatens him with vengeance or suicide as another woman in her situation might do. Even though she knows that she has lost him after he leaves, in her letter to him she still bares her heart. Her love and hope are manifested in the gifts that accompany her letter, all carefully chosen to symbolize her feelings:

The jade ring I am sending to you has been my fondest personal possession since my childhood. Jade is symbolic of integrity and constancy. The endless circle of the ring signifies continuity. I am also sending you a skein of silk thread and a tea-grinder made of speckled bamboo. These articles are valueless in themselves; they merely convey my hopes that your love may be as true and firm as jade, and as endless as the ring. The speckles on the bamboo will remind you of my tears; the skein of silk, my tangled feelings and confused thoughts about you. . . .[18]

Several passages describe in detail Ying-ying's many talents and her characteristic traits. She may be capricious and enigmatic at times, but there is nothing in her words or action that could justify Chang's fear that she might change into "something monstrous." Chang's groundless fears and suspicions, if they are to be understood as real, may stem from her over-generosity and his own active imagination. To the modern eye, Ying-ying may seem to be too meek and too submissive. Yet as a victim of a male-dominated society with its double moral standard, Ying-ying emerges not as a conventional woman but as a believable rebel with an exceedingly strong personality and invincible moral stamina. Chang may be the scandalous seducer who both ignites and terminates the love affair that destroys her (and most likely his own) happiness, but she is not the helpless victim of his seduction. She rejects and accepts him of her own free will. Even when she is deserted in the end, she is still able to pick up the pieces and make the best of her life, and she manages to tell him off when he tries to disturb her after she is married to another man. Witness the following poem she writes to him after she refuses to see him:

> Since I have been wasting away with my beauty gone,
> Tossing and turning endlessly, I hate to leave my couch.
> It is not because of others I am ashamed to rise;
> For you I have suffered, for you I am ashamed.[19]

The hurt is still there, the memory remains, but there is no rancor. If in this poem she is still egocentric and slightly sardonic, in the following poem, which decisively terminates the romance, her attitude has shifted from the hurt ego position to that of the superego. Practical and level-headed, she has become altruistic. She is thinking more of their respective mates when she writes to Chang for the last time:

> Since you have abandoned me
> What more is to be said?

> Yet once did you love me
> As dearly as life itself.
> Better now turn those old feelings
> Into love for your own mate.[20]

The character of Ying-ying comes more fully alive and is far superior to that of Chang. Chang, who is introduced to us as a man of propriety, falls far short of our expectations, whereas Ying-ying, who is rejected by her lover because he suspects that she might be a bad influence on him, remains constant in her love but outgrows her self-pity. Nothing short of intended irony could justify such an unbalanced treatment of the two main characters, or the reversal of our normal expectations. Moreover, that the author intends the reader to recognize the ironic mode is suggested by his choice of words. The word *chen*, which I have translated as "immortal" or "fairy," has a more literal meaning: namely, "truth" or "reality." One senses an element of sarcasm in Chang's attempt to justify his abandonment of the "true" or the "real" in moral terms. And the word propriety, *li*, the Confucian moral principle, which appears frequently in the narrative, can be taken as another ironic indication of the author's explicit intentions.

In view of the autobiographical evidence in the story, elsewhere substantiated by some of Yüan Chen's farewell poems,[21] we may even go so far as to suggest that the author is consciously or subconsciously ashamed of the hero or antihero (i.e., himself in disguise) for this act of desertion. Thus, he presents his protagonist in so incongruous a manner that the discerning reader cannot fail to detect the satirical mode implied in the narrative. On the other hand, his sympathy for Ying-ying motivates him to idealize her, so that he emphasizes her moral strength and constancy in contrast to that of her lover. For the sake of self-preservation or convention, however, he tries to cover up Chang's weakness and immorality with a false moral justification, which in turn suggests an even greater irony. There is an ironic twist in Chang's defense of his own actions; not only can this be taken as self-criticism but also as social criticism—he satirizes not only himself but also the social mores of his times that force him to abandon the real for such illusory gains as social approval and political success. Viewed in this light, one may conclude that Yüan Chen's prose fiction, like Ying-ying, has its flaws, but that it remains an "extraordinary creation" and a literary enigma. Only a work possessing timeless artistic qualities can afford several levels of interpretation and continue to arouse interest and challenge the reader's imagination.

CHAPTER 7

Conclusion

HAVING examined briefly the historical evidence relating to Yüan Chen's life and scrutinized some of his works in the preceding chapters, I would like to formulate some personal impressions and offer my own assessment of the poet. Although my views may be as subjective as those of others, I hope a few new vistas may be opened through my explorations, so that this long-neglected T'ang poet may be better understood.

Public opinion has a way of affecting one's reputation and vice versa. Yüan Chen's true worth as a poet, however, must not be gauged by public opinion or by his literary reputation alone, because frequently the two tend to contradict each other. In one instance, it was rumored that Yüan Chen attained high office merely through the strength of his poetry, ignoring the fact that he had to pass the government examinations at three different levels before he gained access to the imperial court. While rumors of this kind stemmed from his reputation as a poet and offset the opposite opinion that his literary reputation was exaggerated as a result of his elevated political status, they nevertheless cast doubts on his reputation as a competent statesman, which he professed to be.

Historically, Yüan Chen has been presented as a man with a keen native intelligence, a razor-sharp wit, an impetuous temper, and a tactless outspokenness. His literary talent and forthright recommendations for governmental reform won him imperial recognition but incurred the hostility of colleagues and superiors in court; his advocacy of peace policies placed him in a camp opposite to an influential faction of court officials; his exposure of corruption in local government was feared and hated by those in power, who used devious means to block if not totally destroy his political career.

Yüan Chen's first political setback came when his political

career had barely begun. Because of his "Ten Point Proposal," he suffered the disgrace of demotion and banishment, and even imprisonment, as he mentioned in one of his poems. He was again banished to the provinces because of his exposure of wrongdoers in local government who enjoyed powerful political connections. There is reason to believe that his removal from the office of chief minister and his final banishment from court were caused, at least in part, by malicious rumors fabricated and spread by his enemies that he had plotted to assassinate his fellow chief minister, P'ei Tu. Although the charge of his involvement in the alleged plot proved to be groundless upon investigation, the damage to his reputation was irreparable, for suspicions about his motivations and his personal character were formed. And these suspicions eventually hardened into conclusions drawn by official historians who were not free from personal bias. Yet views recorded in official histories do carry the insignia of authority, which is seldom questioned and easily accepted by posterity. Representative of modern scholars who share this historical bias is Howard S. Levy, who, in contrasting Yüan Chen with Po Chü-i, observes:

The literary outlook of the two men was so similar that there were references to them in the T'ang as Yüan-Po, but Confucian-oriented historians viewed them quite differently in relating their written advocacies to social-political behavior. Po was considered superior to Yüan in adhering to the ideals he professed while Yüan was criticized as having been a sham Confucian. The *New T'ang History* critique points out that, while Yüan Chen spoke about ideal government, he immersed himself in political factionalism from start to finish and led a frivolous life. A Japanese scholar who noted this discrepancy in treatment believed it must have stemmed from Yüan Chen's desire to achieve political prominence, a desire so great that he was ready to avail himself of any and all chances to become a chief minister. Po Chü-i, by contrast, adhered to the ideals he had professed in earlier years and remained untouched by cliquishness and political factionalism. Thus his political and moral behaviors were correlated much more closely and he avoided becoming an object of derision.[1]

As I have indicated earlier, one false impression leads to another, and what might very well have begun as an attempt to discredit Yüan Chen's character for purposes of political advantage was later taken as a matter of fact. Speculations that Yüan Chen was a professing but unprincipled Confucian bent on obtaining political power without regard for moral principle, as suggested by the Japanese scholar (Yokoyama) mentioned above by Levy, is not supported by solid evidence.[2] Nevertheless, this attitude has been adopted by many critics and literary historians both in the East and in the West. As a consequence, the literary merits of Yüan Chen the poet have at times been beclouded by the public image of Yüan Chen the man, whose personal character has been the subject of criticism. In addition, Yüan Chen himself may have contributed to his own notoriety because of "The Story of Ying-ying," in which he presents the male protagonist in an unfavorable light. Generally believed to have been written by Yüan Chen on the basis of personal experiences, this work, which has immortalized its author, has also ironically discredited him on moral grounds. For the undiscerning reader has tended to confuse the behavior of the fictional hero of the story with that of the author himself. Consequently, some critics have interpreted every move Yüan Chen made in his life, either public or private, as being motivated by a desire to achieve "political prominence," including that of marriage.[3]

A close examination of Yüan Chen's works and those of his friends, however, yields a rather different picture of the man. Politically, he espoused Confucian ideals, and there is much in the record of his official career to substantiate the conclusion that he followed those principles in practice. That he was later unable to realize all of his youthful ideas, such as those enunciated in "The Forest of Plans" on which he collaborated with Po Chü-i, does not seem to have been due to any unwillingness on his part to accomplish them, but rather because of entrenched political interests, factionalism in the bureaucracy, and policy disputes. After he was removed from a position of high influence where he could act on behalf of the general populace, he continued to work in a more limited way for the alleviation of public ills in the outlying districts.[4]

Yüan Chen's faith in the didactic, pragmatic function of literature remained with him throughout his life. When he was unable to implement social reforms directly, he resorted to literature as an instrument to rectify government malfeasance and corruption. In order to disseminate his ideas, to redress wrongs, to satirize the powerful, and to admonish or remonstrate with the emperor, he chose to write in a language that was readily understood and appreciated by the greatest number of people. For this reason, he was also opposed to an obscure and ornate literary style. He formulated with his friends a poetical theory that bridged past and present: relating the Confucian utilitarian function of literature to a modified, aesthetically acceptable mode of expression that appeals to a wide audience.

If we have only a sketchy knowledge of Yüan Chen as a public figure, even less is known of his private life. The most reliable information left to us is his writing. Eighteen centuries ago, Ts'ao P'ei (188–227) wrote, "Life and honor are limited by time; glory and happiness are confined to one's lifetime—all reach their inevitable end too soon. Only the good writing one creates remains timeless and everlasting."[5] In the poetry Yüan Chen has left us we can readily find substantial proof that he was a man of integrity and sensitivity, if not always a sensible person.

His friendship with Po Chü-i has become almost legendary. That he was capable of a profound and lasting relationship with a person whose integrity has been traditionally regarded as above reproach should help to dispel any misgivings concerning his own moral character. Levy's suggestion that in later life Po Chü-i cooled toward Yüan Chen because "Yüan conspired with the eunuchs in trying to become minister" is not supported by the available evidence.[6] Although the two seldom spent any length of time together after their respective exiles from the capital, they never stopped writing to each other, exhorting each other, and exchanging poems whenever they could, even as late as 829, two years before Yüan Chen's death. The poems exchanged between the two, though many are no longer extant, were, as Po Chü-i stated in the introduction to the second series of his *Collected Works*, close to a thousand in number and collected into sixteen *chüan*.[7] The uniqueness of their friendship was best described by Po Chü-i in his "In Memoriam" to Yüan Chen in 831: "In poverty or in prosperity, it never made any

difference to us. The firmness of gold and stone, the adhesion of
pitch and glue, are not strong enough analogies to depict our
friendship."[8] Again he wrote in 832, a year after Yüan Chen's
death: "My lifelong friendship with the deceased Chief Minister
Yüan could only be terminated by death. It was our respective
karma that our hearts were joined as one."[9]

Some critics interpret Po Chü-i's close friendship with Liu
Yü-hsi in later years as an indication of his disaffection with
Yüan Chen. It seems more likely, however, that Po Chü-i formed
a close relationship with Liu only after the death of Yüan
Chen. Witness Po's own explanation in the collection of poems
he exchanged with Liu Yü-hsi:

> In former days I exchanged numerous poems with Yüan Chen;
> many of them still circulate by word of mouth. I used to say to Yüan
> Chen in jest, "It has been my good fortune as well as my misfortune
> to have you as my friend and poetic rival for more than twenty years.
> It was fortunate for me that we could share our sentiments and
> spread our fame together.... But when the public speaks of literary
> genius they refer to both Yüan and Po. Only because of you I cannot
> excel as the single literary giant striding along the districts of Wu
> and Yüeh. Is not this my misfortune?" Now growing old I again meet
> my match in Liu Yü-shi. Can this be my second misfortune?[10]

One may well wonder if Po Chü-i did not profit more than
he was willing to admit from his friendship with Yüan Chen,
who was seven years his junior but who ranked higher in the
two examinations they took together and who attained higher
political office. Despite the common belief to the contrary, Yüan
Chen seems to have been the first of the two to formulate critical
theories and to experiment with new poetic ideas, as the dates
of their respective letters concerning poetry indicate.[11] Although
Po Chü-i made greater use of the new *yüeh-fu* form than Yüan
Chen, he began to write in that style only after he had seen
poems composed by Yüan Chen and Li Shen, from which examples he drew inspiration. According to Po Chü-i, whenever he
sent his poems to Yüan Chen, he always received in return constructive comment and advice.

If Yüan Chen was of a quicker native wit, Po Chü-i, on the
other hand, was the wiser of the two—he was both more temperate

and more tactful. This is seen in his ability to steer clear of political strife and to maintain a neutral position between opposing political factions. But it was more poetry than politics that cemented their friendship and united their minds. In a letter to Yüan Chen, the older poet writes: "When we are in favorable circumstances, we exchange poems for mutual edification; when we are in adversity, we exchange poems to encourage each other; when we are apart, we write to console each other; when we are together, we write to amuse each other."[12] It may be pointed out that while both men were poets of considerable genius, their mutual criticism and constant exchanges of opinion must have aided each immensely in the development of their respective literary skills.

Even more important, Yüan Chen found in Po Chü-i the one human being who could truly understand him and share with him common social concerns and literary goals. Po was one with whom he could even confide the details of his personal life,[13] and from whom he could receive sympathy and consolation. Indeed, Yüan Chen would not have been misunderstood and become an "object of derision" if the world had paid greater attention to what Po Chü-i said of his friend. In his "In Memoriam" and "Tomb Inscription" for Yüan Chen, Po reveals with specific examples the real character of his friend, whose positive actions were overlooked and whose true motives were impugned by later historians.

If Yüan Chen's success in the political world was limited, as indeed it was, his contributions to Chinese literary heritage were by no means insignificant. He was instrumental in bringing about changes in the prose style of official documents, which in turn must have had a profound impact on prose styles of his contemporaries in general. Thus, directly or indirectly, he assisted the *ku-wen* movement that was then underway. In addition, the example of his prose fiction as a model of lucid expression and verbal precision must also have been far-reaching.

Although Yüan Chen was not a professional literary critic or historian, he was original in his classification of the various subgenres in Chinese poetry, which are much more detailed than those of earlier literary theorists. He was also an astute and daring critic of his predecessors, especially in his critical evaluation of Li Po and Tu Fu. While he allowed his belief in the didactic, utilitarian function of poetry to color his literary criteria, his emphasis on the poet's social responsibility, while not entirely new, was an important corrective to ideals and standards that neglected content in favor of aesthetic appeals. With the help of his poetic coterie, Yüan Chen was able to translate the time-honored classical concept of the nature and function of literature into practice. Social comment and political allegory constitute the main thrusts of his serious poems.

Yüan Chen, however, was not a strait-laced Confucian poet who would allow his social and political ideology to subjugate literary and aesthetic considerations. The language of his poetry may be natural and easy to understand, but it is never dull, and rarely prosaic. Most of his poems are characteristically musical and euphonious, fresh in diction, and innovative in rhythm. As Po Chü-i once commented, Yüan Chen was particularly skilled at using the most difficult rhymes without making the language sound contrived or having his ideas restricted. He is also noted for his originality in the use of poetic imagery. Some of his poetic images remain, after the passage of more than a millenium, sharp and fresh. Even some expressions that have become hackneyed through repeated usage by later poets were oftentimes coined by Yüan Chen. Some contemporary Chinese frequently quote such lines as, "Having seen the sea, I crave no other waters;/ Aside from those by Mount Wu, there is no cloud" (poem 50), without realizing that they are from a poem by Yüan Chen.

Since poetry was not only a social responsibility but also a part of Yüan Chen's life, he wrote poems on practically all occasions, in various moods, and in diverse meters. His narrative poems are as rich in meticulous details as his lyrical poems are effused with emotion. Occasionally, some of his verses are light in tone, and some may even be deemed "frivolous" in subject matter. There seems some justification, then, for the pithy remark by the Sung poet-scholar Su Tung-p'o that "Meng Chiao was frigid (*han*), Chia T'ao, gaunt (*shou*), Po Chü-i, vulgar (*su*), and Yüan Chen, frivolous (*ch'ing*)."[14] These epithets are apropos in some cases, but only a handful of Yüan Chen's romantic poems can truly be considered "frivolous." Variety and versatility are words that perhaps more properly characterize Yüan Chen's poetry. Despite the relatively small number of his poems available to us, they do illustrate the wide variety of subject matter and prosodic patterns characteristic of his poems. More often than not he succeeded in his attempts to invent new rhythms and new forms, to embody profound meaning in simple language, and to create flawless parallelism without sacrificing either sense or feeling.

Surveying his political career and his literary achievements, we come to the conclusion that whatever his personal weaknesses and failings, and whatever his disillusionments in public life, Yüan Chen remained faithful to his commitment to life through his poetry. Although a man of many parts, he should be remembered primarily as a poet. For as a poet he had fulfilled his mission. And poetry was his fulfillment.

Notes and References

For convenience, the most frequently cited journals and Chinese texts are abbreviated as follows. Complete bibliographical data are found in "Selected Bibliography."

CTS	*Chiu T'ang shu* (Old T'ang History)
CTShih	*Ch'üan T'ang shih* (Complete poetry anthology of T'ang)
HJAS	*Harvard Journal of Asiatic Studies*
HTS	*Hsin T'ang shu* (New T'ang History)
JAOS	*Journal of the American Oriental Society*
PSCCC	*Po-shih Ch'ang-ch'ing chi* (Po Chü-i's Collected Works)
SKCS	*Ssu-k'u ch'üan shu* (Complete Libraries of Chinese Works)
SPPY	*Ssu-pu pei-yao* (Essential Collections of Chinese books)
SPTK	*Ssu-pu ts'ung-k'an* (Encyclopedic Collections of Chinese books)
THY	*T'ang hui-yao* (Important Facts and Events of T'ang)
TSCC	*Ts'ung-shu chi-ch'eng* (Collections of sets of Chinese books)
TTC	*Ts'ai tiao chi* (Voices of Geniuses)
YSCCC	*Yüan-shih Ch'ang-ch'ing chi* (Yüan Chen's Collected Works)
YSCCCPY	*Yüan-shih Ch'ang-ch'ing chi pu-yi* (Yüan Chen's Collected Works, Supplement)

Chapter One

1. *CTS* 200A. 15788b-9A; *HTS* 225. 1747a-6b. See also Edwin G. Pulleyblank, *The Background of the Rebellion of An Lu-shan* (London, 1955), chs. 2 & 3; cf. Robert des Rotours, *Histoire de Ngan Lou-chan* (Paris, 1960). Referred to elsewhere in the text as An-Shih Rebellion or An Lu-shan Rebellion.

2. Robert des Rotours, *Le Traité des examens* (Paris, 1932), pp. 205; 209n; *HTS* 44. 16120b-1a.

3. Shun-tsung came to the throne on February 28, 805, and abdicated on August 28 of the same year. Cf. Des Rotours, *Traité des fonctionnaires et traité de l'armée* (Leiden, 1947), vol. 1, p. 352. See also Han Yü, *Shun-tsung shih-lu*, in *Ch'ang-li wen-chi* (Taipei, 1960), *chüan* 6-10, pp. 263–74; Ch'en Yin-k'o, "The *Shun-tsung shih-lu* and the *Hsü hsüan-kuai lu*," *HJAS*, 3 (1938), 9–16.

4. *CTS* 166. 15480a; *HTS* 147. 17145b.

5. Ch'en Yin-k'o, *T'ang-tai cheng-chih shih shu-lun kao* (Peking, 1956), pp. 75–77.

6. *Ibid.,* pp. 71, 74. Cf. Charles A. Peterson, "The Restoration Completed: Emperor Hsien-tsung and the Provinces," in *Perspectives on the T'ang*, ed. A. F. Wright and Denis Twitchett, (New Haven, 1973), pp. 153–58.

7. They are known by their posthumous titles and reign periods as follows: Tai-tsung (763–779); Te-tsung (780–805); Shun-tsung (February-August 805); Hsien-tsung (805–820); Mu-tsung (820–824); Ching-tsung (824–827); Wen-tsung (827–841).

8. For a detailed study of some instances of Yüan Chen's war against government corruption, see Charles A. Peterson, "Corruption Unmasked: Yüan Chen's Investigations in Szechwan," *Asia Minor*, 18 (1973), 34–78.

9. *CTS* 200A. 15793b-6b; *HTS* 225A. 17474a-8b.

10. See Charles O. Hucker, "Confucianism and the Chinese Censorial System," in *Confucianism and Chinese Civilization*, ed. Arthur F. Wright (New York, 1964), pp. 50–76.

Chapter Two

1. *CTS* 166. 15480a.; *YSCCC, chüan* 58, p. 663.

2. *CTS* 166. 15480a; *YSCCC,* ch. 57, p. 657.

3. *YSCCC,* ch. 57, p. 657.

4. *PSCC,* ch. 25, pp. 130, 131.

5. *YSCCC,* ch. 11, p. 131.

6. *Ibid.,* ch. 58, pp. 663–66.

7. *Ibid.,* ch. 30, p. 379.

8. *Ibid.,* ch. 30, p. 377.

9. Ch'en Yin-k'o, *Yüan Po shih chien cheng-kao,* rev. ed. (Taipei, 1963), pp. 106–16; see also Chapter 6 of the present volume.

10. Han Yü, *Ch'ang-li wen-chi* (Taipei, 1960), ch. 25, p. 181; Ssu-ma Kuang. *Tzu-chih t'ung-chien,* 237, 7630–33.

11. *THY* 75. 1380.

12. *PSCC,* ch. 45, p. 236.

13. The work is no longer extant but is cited by Po Chü-i in the

introduction to his "Tomb Inscription of Yüan Chen," *PSCCC, ch.* 61, p. 337.

14. *THY, ch.* 76, p. 1389.

15. *PSCCC, ch.* 45, 46, 47, 48.

16. *Ibid., ch.* 45, p. 236.

17. The term *shih-yi* means "to pick up what was omitted." Thus, Arthur Waley translated it as "omissioner," which is rather quaint but is more accurate perhaps than the term "imperial censor," which designates a more important official role. Cf. Eugene Feifel, *Po Chü-i as a Censor* (The Hague, 1961), p. 23n.

18. The term *ch'ing-yün* means, literally, "blue cloud." It has been a generally accepted symbol for edifying ambition (with moral and political overtones). Possibly *ch'ing-yün* is identical with the blue sky beyond the clouds, which stands for the ultimate goal of all aspiring scholars. A note to *"Pei-kuan kung-ch'ing piao"* (Chart of Official Titles) in the *Han-shu* (History of the [former] Han dynasty), says that *yün* means certain high-ranking officials, e.g., *ch'ing-yün* stands for "spring official" (*ch'un-kuan*), a kind of master of ceremonies in charge of the official spring sacrifice. It is used more figuratively here, as in the *Huai-nan-tzu* 15:8b (SPTK): "Ambition excessive as the blue cloud."

19. *CTS* 166. 15481a; *HTS* 174. 17147a.

20. *YSCCC, ch.* 29, pp. 367–71. *CTS* 15480a-1a; *HTS* 174. 17145b-6b.

21. *YSCCC, ch.* 32, p. 405.

22. The arrest is not mentioned in either the *CTS* or *HTS*. Yüan Chen, however, made reference to it in "Listening to Yü Chi-chih Playing the Tune of 'The Crow Caws at Night.'" See poem 71 of this volume on p. 129.

23. *CTS* 166. 15481a.

24. Han Yü, *Ch'ang-li wen-chi, ch.* 24, p. 180.

25. *CTS* 166, 15481a; *HTS* 174. 17146b. Cf. also Peterson, "Corruption Unmasked."

26. Feifel, *ch.* 15, pp. 156–63.

27. *Ibid.*

28. *CTS* 166. 15481b; *HTS* 174. 17147a.

29. *Ibid.*

30. Cf. *PSCCC, ch.* 43, p. 230–31.

31. *YSCCC, ch.* 33, pp. 415–17.

32. *CTS* 166. 15482a; *HTS* 174. 17147a.

33. *PSCCC, ch.* 61, pp. 337–38.

34. Howard S. Levy, *Translations from Po Chü-i's Collected Works*

(New York, 1971), vol. 1, p. 6; Wang Shih-yi, *Po Chü-i* (Shanghai, 1957), p. 104.

Chapter Three

1. *YSCCC, chüan* 30, p. 377.

2. *Ibid., ch.* 28, pp. 355–56.

3. *Ibid.,* p. 357.

4. *Ibid.,* pp. 359–60.

5. *Ibid.,* pp. 362–64.

6. The *fu* is a literary genre which is a hybrid of poetry and prose. It was derived from the *sao* form of poetry first made famous by the *Li-sao* ("Encountering Sorrow"), attributed to Ch'ü Yüan of the fourth century B.C. The early *fu* is generally regarded by the Chinese as a subgenre of poetry. But some translators call it "prose-poetry" and others, "poetic prose." For detailed discussion, see David R. Knechtges, *The Han Rhapsody; A Study of the Fu of Yang Hsiung* (53 B.C.–18 A.D.) (New York & London, 1976), pp. 12–43; Burton Watson, *Chinese Rhyme-Prose* (New York, 1971), pp. 1–18. For *p'an,* see Arthur Waley, *The Life and Times of Po Chü-i* (London, 1949), p. 28.

7. *YSCCC, ch.* 29, p. 372. The Duke of Chou and Duke of Shao were both kinsmen of Wu Wang, founder of the Chou dynasty (1177–256 B.C.). They were loyal ministers who assisted Wu Wang's young heir during his early reign.

8. *Ibid., ch.* 29, pp. 368–69.

9. *Ibid.,* p. 369.

10. *Ibid.,* pp. 370–71.

11. *CTS* 166. 15481a; *HTS* 174. 17146b.

12. *YSCCC, ch.* 32, p. 405. See also the translated version in Arthur Waley, *The Life and Times of Po Chü-i* (London, 1949), p. 42.

13. *YSCCC, ch.* 37, p. 453. For an English version of Yüan's memorial see Peterson, "Corruption Unmasked," pp. 72–78.

14. *YSCCC,* pp. 453–57 *et passim.*

15. *Ibid.,* pp. 461–62. Cf. also Peterson, "Corruption Unmasked," pp. 77–78.

16. *Ibid., ch.* 38, pp. 467–68.

17. *Ibid.,* p. 468.

18. No document impeaching Fang Shih or reporting his malfeasance is included in Yüan Chen's works. Nor did Fang Shih's biographers in the *CTS* and *HTS* mention anything related to his dismissal as mayor by Yüan Chen; cf. *CTS* 111. 3501; *HTS* 139. 3986. See also Feifel, pp. 158–59.

19. For the English translation of Po Chü-i's memorial, see Feifel, pp. 238–41.

20. Yüan Chen continued his practice of sending memorials to the throne on behalf of the common people in his district, requesting reductions in taxes, equalization of land ownership, and discontinuance of shipping seafood to the capital as local tribute, etc. (See *YSCCC, ch.* 39.)

Chapter Four

1. Ezra Pound, *Polite Essays* (London, 1937), p. 167.

2. *Ibid.,* pp. 167–77 *et passim.*

3. For a comprehensive discussion of the *ku-wen* movement, see Cheng Chen-to, *Chung-kuo wen-hsüeh shih* (Peking, 1932), pp. 478–91; cf. also James Liu, *Chinese Theories of Literature* (Chicago, 1975), p. 27, in which Liu uses "Archaic Prose" for *ku-wen,* and "Parallel Prose" for *p'ien-wen.*

4. William H. Nienhauser, Jr., et. al., *Liu Tsung-yüan* (New York, 1973), p. 20.

5. A schematic prose characterized by its parallel structures and balanced tonal antithesis. For a description of *p'ien-wen* see James R. Hightower, "Some Characteristics of Parallel Prose," in *Studies in Chinese Literature,* ed. John L. Bishop, (Cambridge, 1965), pp. 108–39; cf. Liu, p. 21.

6. Lo Ken-tse, *Chung-kuo wen-hsüeh p'i-p'ing shih* (Shanghai, 1957), vol. 2, p. 113. See also Chauncey S. Goodrich, *Biography of Su Ch'o* (Berkeley, 1953), for a translation of *chüan* 23 of the *Chou-shu.*

7. *Sui-shu, ch.* 66. 11850a-2b.

8. Cf. Ch'en Yin-k'o. *Yüan Po shih-chien cheng-kao,* pp. 107–16.

9. Most translators prefer the title *Ying-ying chuan* (because it is easy to translate) to *Hui-chen chi,* which may mean either "Meeting with a Fairy" or "Encountering an Immortal."

10. It is included in *T'ai-p'ing Miscellany* (*T'ai-p'ing kuang-chi*) *ch.* 488 under the title: "*Ying-ying chuan.*" For its influence on later Chinese literature, see C. T. Hsia's "Critical Introduction" to S. I. Hsiung, tr., *The Romance of the Western Chamber* (New York, 1968), pp. xi–xxxii.

11. Ch'en Yin-k'o, *Yüan Po shih-chien cheng-kao,* p. 115. Han Yü's "*Mao Ying chuan*" was written in imitation of Szu-ma Ch'ien's famous *Historical Records* (*Shih-chi*) as an exemplification of the classical prose style. Yüan Chen's prose fiction seems to be an imitation of the style of the *Tso Chronicles* (*Tso-chuan*), and it is more

successful as a work of art, possibly because of its autobiographical elements and intimate emotions. Han Yü's prose fiction, on the other hand, is a playful exercise, sketchy, and lacking in attention to detail.

12. "The Charge to Fu Yüeh," in the "Book of Shang," Book VIII of the *Shu-ching*; cf. *The Chinese Classics*, trans. by James Legge, (Hong Kong, 1865–1895), vol. III, pp. 249–63. Rpt. Hong Kong, 1960.

13. "The Punitive Expedition of Yin," in "The Book of Hea," Book IV of the *Shu-ching*; cf. Legge, vol. III, pp. 162–71.

14. See note 6, Chapter Three.

15. *YSCCC, ch.* 40, pp. 483–84.

16. *Ibid.*, p. 484.

17. *CTS* 166. 15490a; *HTS* 174. 17147a; cf. also *PSCCC, ch.* 61, p. 337.

18. Quoted in Hu Yün-yi, *T'ang-shih yen-chiu* (Hong Kong, 1959), p. 33.

19. *Ibid.*, pp. 33–34.

20. *Ibid.*

21. John Wu, *The Four Seasons of T'ang Poets* (Rutland, Vermont, and Tokyo, 1972). In this book, important T'ang poets are grouped under the four seasons, each of which is supposed to purport the mood and temper characterizing their poetry.

22. *Ibid.*, p. 28.

23. *YSCCC, ch.* 60, pp. 689–90.

24. Cf. Hideki Hanabusa, *Haku Kyo-i kenkyu* (Tokyo, 1971), pp. 201–10.

25. *YSCCC, ch.* 60, p. 690.

26. *PSCCC, ch.* 52, p. 283, "Introduction to Twenty-Three Poems Written to Harmonize with Yüan Chen's Poems (written in 828)." The passage is quoted from Arthur Waley, *The Life*, p. 172.

27. *YSCCC, ch.* 51, p. 602.

28. *Ibid.*

29. *Ibid.*

30. *Ibid.*, p. 605.

31. Tuan Ch'eng-shih, *Yu-yang tsa-tsu* (Shanghai, 1929), *ch.* 8, p. 60, [*Ts'ung-shu chi-ch'eng* collectiana].

32. *YSCCC, ch.* 60, p. 690.

33. *Ibid.*

34. Cf. Hans H. Frankel, "*Yüeh-fu* Poetry," in *Studies in Chinese Literary Genres* (Berkeley, Los Angeles and London, 1974), ed. Cyril Birch, pp. 69–107.

35. *Ibid.*, p. 70.

36. *YSCCC, ch.* 23, pp. 283.

37. *Ibid., ch.* 24, p. 302.

38. *PSCCC, ch.* 3 and 4.

39. I.e., "Po su Yüan ch'ing," a casual remark first made by Su Tung-p'o (1036–1101), in *Chi Liu Tzu-yü wen yi shou,* which has been widely quoted ever since. *Cf.* Su Shih, *Su Tung-p'o ch'üan chi* (Taipei, 1964), vol. 1, p. 412.

40. *PSCCC, ch.* 3, p. 17.

41. *Ibid., ch.* 28, 143; italics added. This passage is translated by Arthur Waley, *The Life,* p. 107.

42. *YSCCC, ch.* 56, pp. 653–56.

43. A reference to the *Shih-ching.*

44. I.e., "Li-sao" ("On Encountering Sorrow"), generally attributed to Ch'ü Yüan of the fourth century B.C. For a complete translation, see David Hawkes, *Ch'u Tz'u: The Songs of the South* (London, 1959), pp. 21–34.

45. The prototype of the seven character verse form, the *Po-liang* style of poetry, derived its name from the Po-liang Tower. It is believed that at the completion of this building, a dedicatory celebration was held. The Emperor Wu of Han composed a verse in seven character lines, and all the ministers adopted the same meter in their verse to commemorate the occasion, thus establishing a new prosodic pattern.

46. Both Su Wu and Li Kuang were Han generals captured by the Huns. Attributed to them are some excellent poems written in five character lines.

47. *Cheng* stands for that part of the *Kuo-feng* (folksongs) section in The *Book of Poetry* collected from the state of Cheng, whose music, according to Confucius, was seductive and therefore inelegant. Here it may be used as a metonym for the entire section of *Kuo-feng,* as opposed to the *Ta-ya* and *Hsiao-ya* sections, which are more elegant in style.

48. Ts'ao P'ei (187–226), also known as Wen-ti of Wei, was also the author of *Classical Discourses (Tien-lun),* of which an essay on literature (*Lun-wen*) alone is extant. His younger brother, Ts'ao Chih (or Ts'ao Tzu-chien), was specially famous for his five character verse.

49. *YSCCC, ch.* 56. p. 654.

50. *Ibid.,* p. 655.

51. Arthur Cooper, *Li Po and Tu Fu* (New York, 1973), p. 45n.

52. *Ibid.,* p. 19.

53. Waley, *The Life,* p. 109; I have changed his last line, which is mistranslated.

54. Han Yü, *Ch'ang-Li*, ch. 5, pp. 55–56, from the poem "*Tiao Chang Chi*."

55. *YSCCC*, ch. 30, pp. 377–82.

56. *Ibid.*, p. 380.

57. In Po Chü-i's own preface to the second series of his *Works*, which consists of *chüan* 51–70, he mentions that Yüan Chen edited and prefaced his first collection of fifty *chüan*. It is not clear whether it was Po Chü-i or Yüan Chen who arranged the poems under these four categories.

58. *YSCCC*, ch. 23, p. 282.

59. *Ibid.*

60. E.g., the "*Wen-fu*" ("A *Fu* on Literature") by Lu Chi (261–303); *Wen-hsin tiao-lung* ("The Literary Mind and the Carving of the Dragon") by Liu Hsieh (fl. sixth century); and the preface to *Wen-hsüan* (*Anthology of Literature*) by Hsiao T'ung (510–531).

61. Cf. *YSCCC*, ch. 30, pp. 377–82; *ch.* 56, pp. 653–56.

Chapter Five

1. *PSCCC*, *chüan* 61, p. 338.

2. *Ibid.*, p. 337; *HTS* 174. 17147a.

3. *PSCCC*, *ch.* 61, p. 337.

4. *YSCCC*, *ch.* 13, pp. 153–54. Hereafter all citations of poems will be given in the text following the translations in abbreviated form, e.g., *YSCCC* 13/153–54. And all footnotes to each poem will be listed under one number only in the notes, with the numbers of the lines specified for easy identification.

5. *YSCCC*, *ch.* 30, p. 377.

6. *Ibid.*, p. 378.

7. *Ibid.*

8. Tu Mu, *Fan-ch'uan wen-chi*, ch. 9, p. 82 (*Ssu-pu ts'ung-k'an* collectiana 41).

9. Waley's *The Life and Times of Po Chü-i* contains a number of Po's poems in translation, in addition to his earlier translations of Po in *Translations from the Chinese* (New York, 1945); Howard S. Levy's *Translations from Po Chü-i's Collected Works*, in two volumes, is also based "on a close reading of Po Chü-i's poetry."

10. Cf. Ch'en Yin-k'o, *Yüan Po*, ch. 3, pp. 61–80 et passim. Wu Yüan-chi was not captured until the twelfth month in 817.

11. *Ibid.*

12. Hung Mai, *Jung-chai shih-hua* IV, quoted in Ch'en Yin-k'o, *Yüan Po*, p. 61.

13. *Kuei-fei* ("honored imperial concubine") was the title con-

ferred upon Yang, whose given name was Yü-huan and who was also known by her religious name T'ai-chen, which is used in the poem.

14. *CTS* 166. 15481b; *HTS* 174. 17147a.

15. [Poem 1] Line 3: "Double-flowering" is a loose translation for the original *ch'ien-yeh t'ao* (literally, "thousand-leaved peach"), which is also known as *pi-t'ao* ("jade peach"). I have adopted this translation in order to be consistent with the imagery of the "red showers" [of petals] in line four. Lines 7–8: The "Grand Emperor" refers to the Hsüan-tsung emperor (r. 713–755), whose romantic story with Yang Kuei-fei has been the inspiration of many literary masterpieces. Line 13: The "Feast of Cold Food" (*han-shih*) comes one hundred-odd days after the winter solstice. Its origin is described in the *Tso Chronicle*, which narrates the story of the recluse Chieh Chih-t'ui of the Warring States period. It is said that Duke Wen of Chin heard of Chieh's reputation and asked him to assist him in government. When he refused, the duke ordered the forest where the recluse lived set afire in order to force him out. Chieh, however, chose to die in the flames rather than serve against his will. To commemorate his death, the Feast of Cold Food was instituted, during which time the use of fire was prohibited. Line 16: Master Ho refers to Ho Chih-huai, a famous *p'i-p'a* (a Chinese string instrument often mistranslated as a lute) player during Hsüan-tsung's reign. Line 17: Eunuch Kao is Kao Li-shih; Nien-nu was a celebrated courtesan during the *t'ien-pao* era, known especially for her fine singing voice. Line 24: For Prince Pin the original note reads, "Young Lord Number Twenty-five," i.e., the twenty-fifth son of Hsüan-tsung. Line 25: Liang-chou, a city on the western border of China, was noted for its foreign influences. The music from Liang-chou was so popular that by the eighth century it was adopted as court music. Line 26: *Chiu-tzu* is a Chinese translation of Kuchah, a country in central Asia. Line 27: Li Mu was a famous composer and flute player of the eighth century. According to one of many legendary anecdotes about Hsüan-tsung, once, during the lantern festival, he and Yang Kuei-fei went incognito into the streets of Lo-yang. Suddenly, a familiar tune was heard coming from a tavern. The emperor recognized it to be a piece he had recently composed for the court musicians. On the following day he had the flute player brought to him for interrogation. The young musician (i.e., Li Mu) confessed that one night, while enjoying the moon on the bridge of Tientsin, he overheard the music coming from the palace walls and wrote it down on the bridge railing, and later played it in the tavern. The emperor was so impressed with Li's musical talent that he dismissed the case. Line 31: Prince Ch'i (i.e., Li Fan) and Prince Hsüeh (i.e.,

Li Yeh) were both younger brothers of Hsüan-tsung. Line 32: The Yang sisters were cousins of Yang Kuei-fei; all three received royal titles and imperial favors. I have translated the term *tou-feng* "raced with the wind" to cover both the literal and symbolic meanings of the term. An alternate rendering would be "compete in beauty," or "strived for influence or popularity," since the word *feng* (wind, air, fad, or influence) is rich in connotations. Line 41: There seems to be a slight discrepancy here in the number of emperors. Since the poem, though undated, must have been written between 815 and 818 (Ch'en Yin-k'o has fixed the date of composition in 817), there would only be five emperors, counting Hsüan-tsung as the first, because the sixth in succession would have been Mu-tsung (r. 821–824), who had not yet come to the throne. It is possible to attribute this discrepancy to scribal error. But some critics have suggested that the text may have been tampered with by the eunuch Ts'ui T'an-chün, before he submitted it to the new emperor in 821. A more plausible explanation would be that since the narrator is supposed to be an ignorant octogenarian, he could not possibly have kept up with the quick succession of emperors that took place during his lifetime. In that case, the "error" would be intentional on the part of the poet to indicate the faulty memory of the old rustic. Line 44: The construction of Hsüan-wu lou began during Te-tsung's reign (780–804). It was intended to house the imperial guards. Hua-o lou was erected by Hsüan-tsung for his brothers as an expression of brotherly love. Yüan Chen could possibly be referring to these two buildings to imply that in Hsien-tsung's reign there was a tightening of security and a lack of brotherly love in the imperial family. Lines 55–56: Both the snakes and the mushrooms may represent evil forces in government. Line 57: Tuan-cheng lou was actually located in the Hua-ch'ing Palace, an imperial lodge on Mount Li, south of T'ung-chou in Shensi; it was famous for its hot springs. This was the palace, not Lien-ch'ang Palace, that Hsüan-tsung and Yang Kuei-fei historically frequented. The mention of Tuan-cheng lou seems to be simply a device to lend authenticity to the story created by the poet. Line 69: Yao Ch'ung (650–721) was president of the Ministry of War during the early years of Hsüan-tsung's reign. Sung Ching (662–737) was minister of state about the same period. Line 75: The *k'ai-yüan* era was followed by the *t'ien-pao* era, which showed a marked decline in Hsüan-tsung's reign. Line 78: Madame Kuo, or Lady Kuo, was one of the three Yang sisters. Line 80: i.e., Yang Kuo-chung (d. 755), cousin of Yang Kuei-fei; Li Lin-fu (d. 752) was of imperial extraction and became the president of the Ministry of Rites through his friendship with another imperial concubine before Yang

Kuei-fei came into favor. Line 84: The rebellion in Wu was led by Li Ch'i, and that in Shu, by Liu P'i. Both rebellions were quelled about 815. Line 85: The rebel leader of Huai-hsi was Wu Yüan-chi, captured in the twelfth year of the *yüan-ho* period, i.e., 817.

16. [Poem 2] The title is derived from an old *yüeh-fu* song. Yüan Chen uses it to retell the story of the downfall of the state of Chao during the period of the Warring States. Line 3: Since his youth, Chao Kua thought of nothing but war, to the dismay of his father, a great general of the state of Chao, who prophesied that his son would bring about the downfall of the state. When war broke out between the states of Chao and Ch'in, Chao Kua was given the command of the army upon the death of his father. Kua's mother protested to the Prince of Chao and revealed her husband's prophecy, but to no avail. The army of 450,000 men led by Chao Kua was totally destroyed by Ch'in troops under the command of Pai Ch'i, a military strategist (*The Historical Records* 73.2331). Line 11: White garments and hemp were worn by the bereaved.

17. [Poem 5] This translation is in *Sunflower Splendor*, eds. W. C. Liu and Irving Lo (New York, 1975), p. 221.

18. [Poem 6] This new *yüeh-fu* title was first used by Li Shen and Yüan Chen, and later by Po Chü-i. After the fifth year of the *t'ien-pao* era (746), when Yang Kuei-fei won the undivided devotion of Hsüan-tsung, all the palace ladies distinguished for their beauty were sent off to live in secluded palaces. Shang-yang was one of six such palaces. There they grew old and died without ever being visited by the emperor. Line 1: "Beauty scout" is my own version of the Chinese term *hua-niao-shih*, meaning literally "flower-bird envoy." Line 21: Hsing-ch'ing was the name of the "Southern Palace," which was traditionally occupied by the crown prince. A criticism of the successors of Hsüan-tsung who continued the same custom is implied here. Lines 28–29: An open criticism of the early T'ang emperors who chose to enfeoff the heir of the Sui dynasty, which preceded the T'ang, rather than employ their own brothers. Line 30: This is an explicit plea to the emperor to allow palace women to be married to princes of low rank.

19. [Poem 8] An alternate title would be "A Merchant's Music," because the same character *lo* (happiness, or joy) may also be read *yüeh* (music). Line 30: In one version, instead of *shih* (gem or stone), the character *chu* (pearls) from the preceding line is repeated. Since both Ching-chou and Heng-yang are districts in the Chinese interior, the word "gems" makes much better sense. Line 58: *Tung-liang* ("beams and pillars") is a conventional term for "pillars of state," and, by extension, "high-powered officials." It may

not be too far-fetched to suggest that the lumberman, the elder son of the rich merchant, had connections with government officials of high rank. Lines 59–60: Salt was a government-controlled commodity in T'ang times. It would have been illegal to trade in salt without paying taxes. Line 64: "Teeth" may also connote "bodyguards" or "hatchet men." Line 68: *Ch'ien-tao* literally means "money-knife," because the earliest form of money in ancient China was coined in the shape of knives.

20. Cf. Edward H. Schafer, "The Auspices of the T'ang," *Journal of the American Oriental Society* 83 (1963), 197–225 et passim.

21. [Poem 9] "Big-billed crow" (*ta-tsui wu*) belongs to the family of *Corvus Coronoides* which is identified by Schafer as the North China Jungle Crow, which is noted for its rapacity (Cf. *Ibid.*). The poet uses it to symbolize evil ministers and in particular powerful eunuchs. The entire poem consists of eighty-eight lines. I have translated only the first half of the poem, because the second half is repetitious. Line 32: According to the commentary to the chapter on "Reptiles" in *Erh-ya* (the earliest glossary of the Chinese language), "The turtle is called sacred, because its back is shaped round like heaven or the firmament, its underside is square like the earth, and the patterns on its shell are modeled after the constellations. It can foretell good and evil fortune." Another source, the *Records of Marvels* (*Shu-yi lun*), states that a turtle of five thousand years of age is known as the "sacred turtle." Line 44: The phoenix stands for the emperor.

22. [Poem 10] Line 1: Te-tsung reigned 780–805. At the beginning of his reign, the northeastern provinces revolted against the central government. The revolt continued for five years. Like his forebear, Hsüan-tsung, during the An Lu-shan Rebellion, Te-tsung also fled to Szechwan when Ch'ang-an was captured by the rebels. The terms "graced" and "visits" are euphemisms for the imperial flight to Szechwan. Line 7: The poet has a note to this line: "Pai-ts'ao is the name of a place in the Lo Valley." Line 8: Ts'ung-t'ung is a town in Szechwan. In a note Yüan Chen quotes a proverb, "To enter Ts'ung-t'ung is as difficult as entering the Yellow Springs." "Yellow Springs" is a Chinese epithet for Hades. Line 10: Chu Tzu and Huai Kuang were both rebel leaders during the *yüan-ho* period. Line 12: *Yüan lu*, literally meaning "drakes and egrets," is a classical allusion to loyal ministers and attendants. Line 33: The term "Seven Sages" (*Ch'i sheng*) alludes to the Yellow Emperor and his six wisemen (Fang Ming, Ch'ang Yü, Chang Jo, etc.), who went to the suburb of Hsiang-ch'eng and lost their way. There was no one around for them to ask for directions (cf. "Hsü-wu kuei" chapter in *Chuang-*

tzu chi-chieh, ed. Wang Hsian-ch'ien. Taipei, 1962). Line 34: The "Five Strong" (*Wu ting*) is an allusion to the story in the *Shui-ching chu* (*Water Classic Commentary*): King Hui of Ch'in intended to invade the state of Shu (modern Szechwan), but he did not know how to proceed, due to the treacherous mountain roads. So he had five stone oxen sculptured and gold placed behind the oxen's tails. Soon it was rumored that these stone oxen defecated gold. When the king of Shu heard of this, he dispatched five strong men of his kingdom to Ch'in to fetch the marvelous objects. Ch'in's troops under the command of Chang Yi and Ssu-ma Ts'o invaded Shu on the road widened and flattened by the passage of the stone oxen. Shu fell. Line 36: Chen-fu *hsien* is a district in Szechwan. Line 37: Ch'ing-shan was a government post station high up the cliffs of Mount O-mei in Szechwan. Line 43: Ch'i Ying was a commander of the imperial guards during Te-tsung's reign. Line 44: Yen Chen was provincial governor of Shu at the time of the imperial flight. Line 45: The *t'ien-pao* period (742–755) during Hsüan-tsung's reign witnessed the An Lu-shan Rebellion. Line 49: General Li (Li Ling-kung) was the military commander whose personal courage and prowess quelled the rebels who captured Ch'ang-an, so that Te-tsung could return to the capital shortly after his flight. Line 78: Hsiang Yü (233–202 B.C.), general of the state of Ch'u, was known to have had an unusually spirited dappled horse. After his defeat by Liu Pang, the founder of the Han dynasty, Hsiang Yü committed suicide. According to legend, his horse galloped into the sea, turned into a dragon and disappeared. Line 81: Ch'in was the ancient name of Shensi province, where Ch'ang-an (modern Sian) was located.

23. [Poem 12] The dodder plant (*Cuscuta chinensis*) is also called the "love vine"; it is a parasitical vine that clings to other plants for sustenance.

24. [Poem 13] Line 13: Citrus trees cannot survive in a cold climate. The "river" is the Yangtse River, which serves as an isotherm marking the change of climate between north and south China. Line 14: Possibly the high altitude prevents raccoons from crossing Mount Wen (also known as Min Shan), which is the central peak in the mountain chain that joins Mount O-mei in the south and Mount Wu in the east. Line 30: *Chi-yang,* literally meaning "striking the earth," is believed to be an ancient game comparable to ninepins. The "Song of Chi-yang" is traditionally assigned to the reign of Emperor Yao (d. 2258 B.C.), the first legendary sage ruler of China's Golden Age. It is said that when Emperor Yao went on an inspection tour he heard an old man sing the following verse that came to be known as "Song of Chi-yang:" "Sun up to work;/ Sun down to rest;/

I till the field for food;/ I dig the well for drink./ Imperial power—/ What is it to me?"

25. [Poem 14] An alternate translation for "witch" would be "shaman" for the Chinese *wu* (for both male and female). Hua is short for Hua-shan, also known as Mt. T'ai-hua, situated in Shensi province. According to the explanation given in the *Erh-ya* on mountains, the mountain south of the Yangtse River is called Hua, and that east of the river is called Yüeh. Both have precipitous cliffs. Lines 26–27: "The Master said, 'Rather than paying court to the occult or the mysterious, I prefer to court the kitchen stove.'" (*The Confucian Analects,* Book IV, chapter 13). Line 28: The Chinese word for "road" is the all-comprehensive word *Tao*. It may mean the physical road on which one travels as well as the metaphysical concept of the "process" or the "way" of nature. Line 30: The emendated text is *"Ch'iu chih tao"* instead of *Ch'iu chih t'ao"* (the latter character with a "wood" radical is obviously a scribal error). It is a direct quotation from the *Confucian Analects* (Book VII, Chapter 34): "The Master said, 'I, Ch'iu, have been praying for a long time!'"

26. [Poem 15] Line 20: Liang Chi (d. 170 A.D.) was a brother of Empress Liang, consort of Emperor Shun of Han (r. 126–145). Shortly after the death of the emperor, Liang Chi poisoned the legitimate heir to the throne and set up a young puppet ruler of his choice, Huan Ti. Later on, Huan Ti, with the help of his loyal ministers, plotted to remove Liang Chi, who subsequently committed suicide. At the time of his death, Liang was the richest man in the entire empire. Line 25: Yao and Shun were the two legendary rulers of China during the "golden age" that preceded the Hsia dynasty (2205–1766 B.C.). Line 29: The "Master" refers to Confucius. Line 31: Lao-tzu, whose name was Li Erh, was supposedly a contemporary of Confucius. He is believed to have been the founder of Taoism. The famous Taoist canon, the *Tao-te ching,* consisting of five thousand words, is traditionally attributed to Lao-tzu. Line 36: *The Rites of Chou (Chou Li)* is also known as the *Chou Kuan (The Institutes of Chou)*; it is generally attributed to the Duke of Chou. The work contains twenty *chüan* (the number "twelve" in the text is undoubtedly wrong). It is one of three texts that form the *Li* or *Book of Rites.* Line 38: Fu Yüeh (1301–1223 B.C.) was the prime minister of Kao-tsung (r. 1324–1265 B.C.) of the Shang-Yin dynasty. *Yüeh ming,* or "Orders to Fu Yüeh" (translated by Legge as "The Charge to Yüeh"), is a chapter in the "Book of Shang" in the *Book of History.* The chapter consists of three parts: the first part relates the dream of Wu Ting, who reigned under the title of Kao-tsung, which leads to the discovery of Fu Yüeh, who becomes prime minister. The second

part consists of the statutes set up by Fu Yüeh after he took office. The third part is a discourse on learning. That which Yüan Chen refers to is most likely the third part. Line 46: The *yu* plant (*Caryopteris divaricata*) is a perennial plant as notorious for its stench as the orchid is famous for its fragrance.

27. Waley, *The Life and Times*, pp. 29, 197 et passim.

28. *Ibid.*, p. 179.

29. [Poem 20] Lines 13–14: This is a reference to Po Chü-i's official duty as *tso shih-yi* in the imperial palace, a post held earlier by Yüan Chen who was now en route to Chiang-ling in the autumn of 810.

30. [Poem 21] Line 13: *Tan-ch'iu*, literally, "vermillion hill," is the name of a mythical locus, a "fairyland," where immortals live and there is no darkness. This is an allusion to a line in the *Ch'u Tz'u* (*Songs of the South*): "I could stay with the winged creatures of *Tan-ch'iu*;/ And remain in the land of immortality." (Cf. "Distant Wanderings" in *Ch'u Tz'u*, V, p. 5).

31. [Poem 22] Lines 1–2: The orange tree may be another reference to a poem by that title in the *Ch'u Tz'u* (Cf. "Nine Declarations," *Ch'u Tz'u*, IV) that is traditionally attributed to Ch'ü Yüan (fl. fourth century B.C.); on the other hand, the two lines together may be taken simply as a description of the autumn scene (Cf. line six of the poem).

32. [Poem 31] Line 2: Hui-chi is the name of a famous mountain in the southeastern part of Shao-hsing, Chekiang province. It is also the name of the prefecture in which the mountain is located.

33. Cf. "In Memoriam to Yüan Chen" (*"Chi Wei-chih wen"*), *PSCCC ch.* 60, p. 334.

34. [Poem 41] Chih-tui was the courtesy name of Po Hsing-chien, younger brother of Po Chü-i and author of a work of prose fiction titled "The Story of Li Wa" (*Li Wa chuan*).

35. The five human relationships in the Confucian context are: sovereign–minister, father–son, elder brother–younger brother, friend–friend, and husband–wife.

36. This anthology is one of the earliest and most comprehensive collections of T'ang poetry ever compiled by a Japanese scholar and was first published privately in 929. Cf. *Nihon hungakushi* (Tokyo: Shibundō, 1966), v. 6. It contains several hundred poems.

37. *PSCCC, ch.* 14, pp. 75–76.

38. *Ibid.*, p. 75.

39. In Yüan Chen's case, the metaphor is ironically ambiguous. Does he compare his first love and mistress or his wife, Ch'eng-chih. with the "plain weave" in the poem?

40. [Poem 42] Line 17: "Black Dragon" is an allusion to the name of a dog belonging to Chang Jan, who, with the help of the dog, escaped assassination at the hand of his wife's lover, according to the *Shou-shen hou-chi*. Line 18: Pi Yü (literally "green jade") is the name of a beautiful girl who was secretly married to Prince Ju-nan of the Liu Sung dynasty (420–478). Line 28: In the unemendated version of the poem, the character *wa*, which I have translated here as "lap dog," has the so-called "female" radical, which is obviously a printing or scribal error as Ch'en Yin-k'o has pointed out in his *Yüan Po shih-chien,* p. 91. Line 29: The girl-servant is believed to be a reference to Ying-ying's maid, Hung-niang, in "The Story of Ying-ying," (cf. Chapter 7). Line 41–42: The poet's own note states that it was "the hair style in vogue," and the shoes are referred to as "the palace footwear style." The latter may also be a reference to P'an Fei, who was consort of the last ruler of the Ch'i dynasty (479–501). It is believed that the king built gold decks in the shape of lotus flowers for her to walk on. Line 43: The poet's note specifies the color of the skirt as being the "color of the lute"; whether he means the string or the wood of the lute is not known. Line 44: According to Ch'en Yin-k'o, *chia-chi*, in the original note, is a dye printing technique invented during the first half of the ninth century. The flower pattern of the print, *ho-huan*, is either *mimosa arborea* or *acacia julibressin*, an auspicious plant which promotes harmony and conjugal bliss. Line 60: A reference to the title of the poem "Hui-chen shih," in "The Story of Ying-ying." Line 67: *Erh-chi* (two cycles) would mean twenty-four years. Yüan Chen was then twenty-three years old, according to the western way of counting age. Line 69: Morning hibiscus, an ephemeral flower, may symbolize his bride, Wei Hui-ts'ung, who died in 809. "Jade pendant" is an allusion to an epithalamium in the *Book of Poetry* (no. 83), see also Legge, tr. *The Chinese Classics* (Hong Kong, 1960). vol. IV, p. 102, and therefore implies his marriage to Miss Wei. Line 70: Lo-fu is an allusion to a beautiful girl in an old *yüeh-fu* song by that title. Line 79: P'an Yüeh was a fifth century poet, who also became a widower when he was young. He is noted for his elegies mourning his wife's death. Line 80: Tutor Hsieh was Hsieh An (320–385), a fabulously wealthy man who was a grand tutor to the heir apparent; here the name stands for Yüan Chen's father-in-law, Wei Hsia-ch'ing, who was also a grand tutor in the later years of his life. Line 82: Gold Valley was an estate near Lo-yang that belonged to Shih Ch'ung (247–300), who was fond of displaying his fabulous wealth. Extravagant festivities were held there during Shih Ch'ung's lifetime. Line 89: Lady Cho (Cho Wen-chün) was traditionally believed to have been

the author of the "White Hair Song" (*Pai-t'ou-yin*). In this song she complained of her husband Ssu-ma Hsiang-ju's infidelity. Line 90: Ah Chiao was the pet name of Empress Ch'en, consort of Han Wu-ti. When Wu-ti was still a child, he was asked by his aunt if he would like to marry Ah Chiao when he grew up. The child answered that if he could marry her, he would build a gold chamber to house her. Although the allusion to "Gold Chamber" identifies Ah Chiao, the real title of the *fu* about Ah Chiao (or Empress Ch'en) is "Fu on the Ch'ang-men Palace" (*Ch'ang-men fu*), composed by Ssu-ma Hsiang-ju on the empress's behalf, when she lost Wu-ti's favor in later years (cf. *Han Wu ku-shih* [*SKCS*] 1.1b). Line 91: Sheng Chi was a favorite of Mu T'ien-tzu (Emperor Mu), who built a jade tower in her honor, and upon her death had her buried beside it (cf. *Mu T'ien-tzu*, ed. Kuo P'u [Taipei, 1966], *chüan* 6.1b.). Line 92: Ming Fei was the posthumous title given to Wang Chao-chün, the palace lady of Han Yüan-ti, who was given in marriage to a *Hsiung-nu* ruler. She died of grief in the alien northland. Legend has it that the grass on her grave in the desert is always green, hence the allusion of "green grave."

41. [Poem 44] Lines 8–9: Chou Fang (780–810) was a T'ang artist celebrated for his portraits of women. The morning clouds may be an analogy to the changeability or unattainability of the beauty of a woman.

42. [Poem 46] Sung Yü (fl. third century B.C.) was a famous poet of Ch'u who wrote the rhymed prose piece, *Teng-t'u fu*. In it he describes a woman of ethereal beauty who lived to the east of his own house. Thus "east of the Sung house" has become an epithet for a woman of surpassing beauty. [Poem 47] Line 4: "Master Jüan" is an allusion to the legend of Jüan Chao and his friend Liu Ch'en of the first century A.D. Gathering herb medicines, they wandered into Mount T'ai, where they met and fell in love with two fairy maidens, who fed them hemp seeds. After what seemed to be six months they returned home. To their consternation, seven generations had passed during their absence.

43. Cf. Ch'en Yin-k'o, *Yüan Po*, p. 88.

44. *Ibid.*, pp. 107–11 et passim.

45. See James R. Hightower, "Yüan Chen and 'The Story of Ying-ying,'" *HJAS*, 33 (1973), 104.

46. [Poem 53] Lines 1–2: The famous folk legend of the "Cow-herd and Weaving Maid" is about two star-crossed lovers who were transformed into two stars: Altair (i.e., the cowherd) and Vega (i.e., the weaving maid). Thus separated by the Sky River (the Milky Way), because they were fated to be apart, the Queen of Heaven

(*Hsi Wang-mu*) took pity on them and allowed them to meet once a year on the seventh day of the seventh month. It was believed that on that day magpies flew to heaven and joined their wings to form a temporary bridge over the Milky Way so that the lovers could be reunited. [Poem 54] Line 6: An allusion to the famous line in the *Book of Poetry* (no. 72): "One day without seeing [my beloved],/ It is like three autumns." Line 9: The Chinese word for "node" is *chieh* (cf. note [line 8] to Poem 21). Line 14: The "broken mirror" is an allusion to Hsü Te-yen of the short-lived Ch'en dynasty (557–587), who married Princess Lo-ch'ang. Before they separated on account of the civil war, the princess broke a mirror, keeping half for herself and giving the other half to her husband to keep like a tally or a token of their pledge at some future reunion. At the fall of the Ch'en dynasty, Princess Lo-ch'ang was captured by Yang Su, founder of the Sui dynasty (589–618). Many years later, Hsü, in search of his wife, came to Ch'ang-an. He put his half mirror on the market for sale, whereby his story was made known to Yang Su, who was so moved by the man's loyalty to his wife that he allowed the couple to be reunited. Line 19: *Huang-ku* is another term for "cowherd." [Poem 55] Line 9: One version has "wild cranes" instead of "wild magpies." The latter is more accurate, because it fits the legend about the magpie bridge in the cowherd–weaving maid legend. The heavenly cock (or rooster) is supposed to announce daybreak every morning with its first crowing.

47. [Poem 58] This is the first of the series of poems under the title "Three Dreams at Chiang-ling." Only two dreams are described in this series, though three dreams are mentioned. Line 15: The daughter of Yüan Chen mentioned in this poem was Pao-tzu, the only child by Wei Hui-ts'ung who survived her mother (cf. Han Yü, *Ch'ang-li wen-chi, chüan* 24). She could not possibly be Fan-tzu, as William Nienhauser has suggested in his translation of the poem in *Sunflower Splendor*. Fan-tzu was born in 816 and died in 819; she was undoubtedly born to Yüan Chen's wife P'ei Jou-chih. Line 43: Ch'ang-an was where his daughter was kept during Yüan Chen's banishment to Chiang-ling in Hupei. Line 50: The stream is a symbol for the mutability of life; cf. *The Confucian Analects* IX, 16: "Standing by a stream, the Master observed, 'All is transient in life like this, unceasing, day and night.'" [Poem 59] Line 2: *Chiung* is a special kind of jasper or jade; cf. Hawkes's translation in *Ch'u Tz'u*; *Songs of the South*, p. 29. Nienhauser has translated it as "coral" in *Sunflower Splendor*, p. 218.

48. See poem 65, which is dated "the night of the fourteenth of the tenth month," i.e., the day after his wife's burial at the ancestral

cemetery in Hsien-yang, the suburb of Ch'ang-an. Yüan Chen was away in Lo-yang and could only imagine her hearse passing along Hsien-yang road.

49. See Poem 58, line 50.

50. In the extant edition of Yüan Chen's *Collected Works,* however, the poem entitled "Dreaming of a Well" has been placed (or misplaced?) before "Three Dreams in Chiang-ling" as an independent poem.

51. [Poem 61] Would it be too far-fetched to suggest that narcissism in the poet is subconsciously revealed in his dream?

52. [Poem 63] Line 1: Most probably, the residence of Yüan Chen's father-in-law was located in this ward in Ch'ang-an. Line 2: The allusion stands for Yüan Chen's father-in-law, who, like Lord Hsieh, also held the title of a grand tutor to the crown prince.

53. [Poem 65] According to Han Yü's tomb inscription for Yüan Chen's wife, she was buried on the thirteenth of the tenth month in 809 (cf. Han Yü, *Ch'ang-li wen-chi, chüan* 6, p. 210).

54. It is significant that this popular anthology of T'ang poetry compiled by Sun Chu (1711–1778) contains only one other poem ("Temporary Palace," a quatrain of twenty characters) besides these three poems.

55. Cf. Ch'en Yin-k'o, *"Yuan Wei-chih 'Ch'ien ch'ien-pei huai' shih chih yuan t'i chi ch'i tz'u-hsu,"* in *Ch'en Yin-k'o hsien-sheng wen-shih lun-chi* (Hong Kong, 1973), vol. 2, pp. 247–59.

56. [Poem 68] Line 1: An allusion to his wife, who was probably the youngest daughter of the Wei family. Line 2: Ch'ien Lou (fl. fifth century B.C.) was a philosopher who lived in poverty. At his death, the shroud was not long enough to cover both his feet and his head. Someone suggested that if the sheet were placed diagonally it would cover the entire corpse. Ch'ien's wife objected, saying that her husband would prefer that it be placed straight, even though insufficient, rather than compromise. [Poem 69] Line 2: The term *pai-nien* (literally "a hundred years") is a euphemism for a lifespan. Line 3: Teng Yu (326 A.D.) was governor of Ho-tung. He fell under the power of the rebel Shih Lo (who assumed the title of king of Chao in the north) and was forced to take office under him. He fled with his family on foot, carrying both his own son and his brother's son on his back. When he was overcome, he abandoned his own son and continued his journey with his brother's son. His reason was that his brother, i.e., his nephew's father, was dead and needed an heir. Since he was still alive he could hope for another son. Unfortunately, he died without leaving an heir. Line 4: P'an Yüeh was a poet of the fifth century A.D., noted for his elegies mourning the

death of his wife. Line 7: "Keeping eyes open forever" refers to the written character *kuan*. It is the name of a special kind of large fish, and it also means "widower." Significantly, the character is composed of a "fish" radical on one side and the picture of an eye over water on the other. The implication is that at the time of the poem's composition the poet intended to remain a widower forever.

57. Ezra Pound, "Canto 76," in *The Cantos* (London, 1960), p. 485.

58. [Poem 71] "The Crow Caws at Night" (*Wu-yeh-t'i*) was a famous tune composed by Wang Yi-ch'ing of the Liu-Sung dynasty (420–478). The circumstances under which the tune was originally composed are related in Yüan Chen's poem. The crow was believed to have been endowed with magic power.

59. [Poem 72] Line 1: A reference to the *Book of Poetry*: "Like the pelicans perching on the beams,/ Their wings are not wet" (*Book of Poetry*, XIV, ii, 2). This metaphor is believed to have been originally used to satirize disloyal and useless ministers at court. It seems that Yüan Chen borrowed this allusion to imply either that he could take the blame for not being able to rid the court of those useless ministers, or that he was responsible if he was being satirized for not having performed his duty well. Line 2: A reference to the anecdote in the *Huai-nan-tzu* 18.6: Sai-weng was an old man who lived at the frontier. When he lost his horse, people commented on his misfortune; but he said, "Who knows that it might not be a blessing in disguise?" A few months later, the lost horse returned with a herd of wild horses, and people commented on his good fortune. The old man said, "Who knows that it might not bring calamity?" One day his young son rode one of his newly acquired horses and fell, breaking his leg. People came to offer condolences. But Sai-weng said, "Who knows that this might not be a blessing?" The following year war broke out and all the young men in his district were drafted and died in the battlefield. The old man's son was spared because of his broken leg. Line 18: *Tushita* (Chinese transliteration: *Tou-shuai*) is a Buddhist term for heaven in which Bodhisattvas reside. Line 19: *Karma* is a Buddhist term of wide application of the principle of universal causality. The principle is also generally linked to destiny, which is controlled by one's actions. For, according to the law of *karma*, every good deed or sin leaves its impression on the soul and remains with it through its present life and goes with it in the future life. Line 25: For P'an Yüeh, see note to line 79 of Poem 42. Line 26: For Teng Yu, see note to line 3 of Poem 69. Line 33: An allusion to an old *yüeh-fu* song by that title which is also its first line. It relates the story of a mother crow which hatched eight

or nine young crows in the rocks of the Southern Mountain but all were killed by the pellets of a man named Ch'in, or men from Ch'in. Cf. *Hsiang-ho ch'ü* 3 in *Yüeh-fu shih chi,* comp. Kuo Mao-ch'ien (tenth-thirteenth c.) [*SPTK* ed.], Shanghai, Commercial Press, 1929. *chüan* 28, pp. 2–3.

60. [Poem 73] *Szu-kuei* literally means "thinking of returning"; it is translated here as "homesick" or "homesickness." Line 20: P'eng-tzu, a mythical character, is the Chinese counterpart of Methuselah. He was the grandson of the legendary King Chuan-hsü (reigned 2513–2435 B.C.) and he lived for seven or eight hundred years. See the "Shuo-lin hsun" in the *Huai-nan-tzu,* ed. Liu An. Taipei: Chunghua shu-chü, 1966 (SPPY ed.). Line 21: Chao Ch'ang was a famous general who died an octogenarian in 815 (cf. *HTS* 170). Line 23: Chiao-chou is the present Ch'ang-wu in Kwangsi, then a region known for malaria. Line 39: During the T'ang times Chiang-ling was a prefecture in the Hupeh province; it belonged to the state of Ch'u during the warring states period. Line 50: The nine classics, i.e., the main Confucian texts, which were augmented in later times by the inclusion of additional titles.

61. [Poem 74] Line 3: Presumably there was an epidemic in Ch'ang-an in the year 815. Line 7: Censor Li's given name is not specified; therefore he is not identifiable.

62. [Poem 75] Verse II, line 1: The poet was stationed in Ch'angsha during his second banishment from the capital. Line 3: The "Fisherman" is a reference to Ch'ü Yüan (fl. fourth century B.C.), who is traditionally believed to be the author of the "Fisherman" (*Yü-fu*) in the *Ch'u Tz'u.* Verse IV, line 3: Jade flower (*Yü-ying*) is a reference to the line in Chiu-chang: "Climbing the K'un-lun Mountain, we ate jade flowers" (*Ch'u Tz'u, chüan* 4, p. 8). Line 5: Ning Ch'i (fl. seventh century B.C.) of the state of Wei retired from public service and became a traveling salesman. Once he lodged outside the eastern gate of the capital of Ch'i. When he saw Duke Huan of Ch'i pass by, he sang a ballad, beating time on the horns of his ox. The duke was greatly impressed with the wisdom expressed in the song and invited him to serve his state, where Ning became a privy councillor. Line 6: Lu T'ung (courtesy name Chieh Yü) was known as "the madman of Ch'u." He feigned madness because he wanted to avoid involvement in a world of turmoil. When he passed Confucius one day, he sang the following verse: "O Phoenix, O Phoenix,/ How is your virtue degenerated!/ Useless is the blame of what has passed./ The future may yet be rescued. Give up! Give up!/ Those who are in politics are hopeless." Confucius tried to speak to Lu T'ung, but he hastened away. Line 7: Sun Teng (fl

third century A.D.), who was seven feet nine inches tall, had a very small mouth. Ch'i-ch'i (i.e., Jung Ch'i-ch'i), a contemporary of Confucius, was noted for his contentment with his lot. Cf. *K'ung-tzu chia-yü* annoted by Wang Su (195–256), 10 *chüan* (*SPTK* ed.), Shanghai: Commercial Press, 1929, *chüan* vi.

63. [Poem 80] Line 5: Hsi Shih (fifth century B.C.) made her living by washing silk in the stream. Her supreme beauty was made known to Kou Chien, king of Yüeh, who had a grudge against the king of Wu. He trained Hsi Shih for three years and then offered her to the king of Wu, who became so infatuated with her that he neglected the affairs of state. Yüeh finally conquered Wu. Line 6: Wei Chieh (286–312 A.D.) was so handsome that he was called "The Jade Person" (*Pi-jen*). Whenever he went out, a crowd would gather to admire his beauty.

64. [Poem 83] Line 1: Chia-ling River begins in Shensi and flows westward through Kansu and southwest Szechwan before it flows into the Yangtse River, which flows eastward into the sea.

65. [Poem 85] This is a literal rendering of the Chinese name *shan p'in-p'a* (*Epigae Asiatica*). It is commonly known as "rock pears" in Japan because of the shape of its fruit. Its flowers are bell-shaped and grow in clusters like those of the rhododendron. Line 15: Lu Chu ("Green Pearl") was the name of a handmaid of Shih Ts'ung (247–300) of the Chin dynasty. She was extraordinarily beautiful and gifted. When Shih Ts'ung was delivered to his enemy, she committed suicide by throwing herself from a tower. Line 16: The Wu-ti emperor of Han had a favorite consort known as Li Fu-jen (Madame Li). She died at a young age. The emperor had a portrait of her painted and installed in the Palace of the Sweet Fountain. A Taoist claimed that he could cause her spirit to appear, if the emperor would perform a certain rite. The emperor complied and saw her for an instant. Line 19: Lo-t'ien was the courtesy name of the poet's friend Po Chü-i. Line 20: Ku-k'ou (literally "mouth of the valley") was another name for Han-chung, which is situated east of Nan-cheng *hsien* in Shensi. Line 32: Fan Hsi (or Fan Ku) is a stream in the southeast of Pao-chi hsien in Shensi. It flows north into the Wei River. It was said that T'ai-kung of Chou was fishing at this stream when he met Wen Wang, the founder of the Chou dynasty (1122–255 B.C.). The line is ambiguous. Yüan Chen here seems to compare himself to the hermit who met Wen Wang, the sage king, and came out of retirement to serve him, i.e., if he could be recognized by his ruler, then those who were in power (*ch'üan-men*) would perhaps groan in fear of his uprightness.

66. [Poem 86] Line 1: T'ao refers to T'ao Ch'ien (365–427), a great poet of nature, especially known for his predilection for chrysanthemums; e.g., "Gathering chrysanthemums by the eastern hedge,/ Distantly I see the southern hills," are famous lines of his.

Chapter Six

1. The term *ch'uan-ch'i* has been translated as "T'ang tales of strange phenomena" by Stephen Owen in *The Poetry of Meng Chiao and Han Yü* (New Haven, 1975).

2. This work is not included in the sixty *chüan* YSCCC, but it is found in a supplementary collection of six *chüan* (YSCCCPY) included in the SKCS as well as in the *T'ang-tai ts'ung-shu*; both under the title *Hui-chen chi*. It is also collected in the *Tai-p'ing Kuang-chi*.

3. *Chieh-yüan* was not Tung's given name, which is unknown; it was the title of a scholar who had passed the preliminary examination in the provinces.

4. Among the translated versions of this story are Waley, *Translations from the Chinese*, pp. 299–313; E. D. Edwards, tr., *Chinese Prose Literature of the T'ang Period* (London, 1938), vol. 2, pp. 190–201; S. I. Hsiung, tr., "The Story of Ts'ui Ying-ying," in *The Romance of the Western Chamber* (London, 1935; rpt., New York, 1968), pp. 271–81; Chi-chen Wang, tr., *Traditional Chinese Tales* (New York, 1944), pp. 75–86; Hightower, "Yüan Chen and 'The Story of Ying-ying,'" pp. 93–103. *Yü-jen*, which I have translated as "precious person," literally means "jade person."

5. That is the *"Hui-chen shih"* from which the story derives its title. This poem is only mentioned by its title. The narrative, however, contains a poem of thirty couplets, titled *"Hui-chen shih; A Sequel,"* by Yüan Chen the narrator, who shows up in the story as the protagonist's close friend. It is the general belief that Yüan Chen's "Sequel" is no other than the *"Hui-chen shih"* mentioned earlier.

6. YSCCCPY, *chüan* 6, p. 9 (SKCS).

7. *Ibid.*

8. See Poem 42.

9. Hightower, "Yüan Chen," pp. 90–123.

10. YSCCCPY, *chüan* 6, p. 5 (SKCS).

11. *Ibid.*, p. 9.

12. Ch'en Yin-k'o, *Yüan Po*, p. 95.

13. Arthur Waley seems to be the only person who rejected Yüan Chen as the author of *"Hui-chen chi"* (cf. Waley, *The Life and Time*, pp. 82, 222, additional notes 70:1).

14. *YSCCCPY, chüan* 6, p. 1.

15. *Ibid.*

16. *Ibid.*

17. *Ibid.,* pp. 2–3.

18. *Ibid.,* p. 6.

19. *Ibid.,* pp. 9–10. My reading of the last two lines differs from other translations. For variant versions, see translations mentioned in note 4 of this chapter.

20. *Ibid.* Waley mistook this poem to be from the protagonist Chang to Ying-ying. If that were the case, Chang would be an even more insensitive villain than he is already shown to be. The confusion lies in the terseness of the Chinese literary style in which pronouns are omitted. However, the narrator, by the use of the adverb "again" (i.e., " *'yu' fu yi chang . . .*"), clearly indicates that this poem is from the same person who sent the previous poem.

21. See Poems 42, 50, 51, 52, 53, 54, 55.

Chapter Seven

1. Cf. Levy, p. 90; Wang Shih-yi, p. 122.

2. In his notes to Chapter 10, Levy refers to Yokoyama Hirō, *Haku Rakuten* (Tokyo: Jinbutsu oraisha, 1967), pp. 248–54; I have not been able to verify the statement.

3. Ch'en Yin-k'o, *Yüan Po,* pp. 110–11.

4. Aside from Yüan Chen's own words, the most reliable source comes from Po Chü-i in his preface to the "Tomb Inscription for Yüan Chen" (*PSCCC, ch.* 61, p. 337). Recently, some scholars have questioned the authenticity of the specific incidents mentioned by Po Chü-i, since they are not found in the biographies of Yüan Chen in the T'ang histories. On the other hand, the compilers of the T'ang histories could very well have purposely left out certain data about Yüan Chen that did not corroborate their personal or the "official" views of the poet.

5. In his critical essay on his contemporaries, "*Lun-wen*" or "*Tien-lun*"; Ts'ao P'ei, *Wei Wen-ti chi* in *Han Wei Liu-ch'ao san-pai chia chi,* ed. Chang P'u (Taipei, 1963), vol. 3 (*chüan* 1, p. 70).

6. Howard S. Levy makes serious unsubstantiated assumptions (Levy, vol. I, p. 6). He does not indicate, however, which of Po's writings support this statement.

7. Po Chü-i's "Postscript" to the second series of his *Collected Works,* in *PSCCC, ch.* 71, p. 396.

8. *Ibid., ch.* 60, p. 334.

9. *Ibid., ch.* 59, p. 329.

10. *Ibid., ch.* 60, p. 332.

11. Yüan Chen's letter to Po Chü-i was written in the early part of 815, whereas Po Chü-i's letter was written toward the end of the same year. Po's response was no doubt prompted by Yüan Chen's letter, which contains his literary essay on Tu Fu and which had been used to preface the tomb inscription he wrote for Tu Fu in 813.

12. *PSCCC, ch.* 28, p. 144.

13. See Po's "Preface to Harmonizing 'Dream of a Spring Excursion' with a Hundred Rhymes," *PSCCC, ch.* 14. pp. 75–76 [*SPTK*].

14. This critical remark was made by Su Tung-p'o in his *"Chi Liu Tzu-yu wen,"* in which he made the cryptic remark about four T'ang poets. It is not certain whether it was the form or content of these individuals' poetry he had in mind. Whatever he meant by the remark, he could not have taken it too seriously, as in many instances he compared himself to Po Chü-i, cf. his ("Poetic Talks"). See Ch'en Yu-ch'in, ed., *Po Chü-i chuan* (Peking, 1962), pp. 39–42. Moreover, no other contemporaries of Su Tung-p'o adhered as seriously to the use of *tz'u-yün*.

Selected Bibliography

PRIMARY SOURCES

Chiu T'ang shu. Comp. Liu Hsu (887–946) et al. In *Erh-shih-ssu shih* (*Po-na* ed.). Taipei: Commercial Press, 1968.

Ch'üan T'ang shih. Comp. Ts'ao Yin et al., under imperial auspices, 1st ed. 1704–1707. 16 vols. Rpt. Taipei: Fu-hsing, 1961.

HAN YÜ. *Ch'ang-li hsien-sheng chi.* 2 vols. (*SPPY* ed.). Shanghai, Chunghua shu-tien, 1927–35.

————. *Han Ch'ang-li ch'üan-chi.* Rpt. Hong Kong: Kuang-chi, n.d.

————. *Han Ch'ang-li wen-chi.* Rpt. Taipei: Shih-chieh shu-chü, 1960.

Hsin T'ang shu. Comp. Ou-yang Hsiu (1007–1072), et al. In *Erh-shih-ssu shih* (*Po-na* ed.). Taipei: Commercial Press, 1968.

Po CHÜ-I. *Po-shih Ch'ang-ch'ing chi.* (*SPTK* ed.). Shanghai, Chunghua shu-chü, 1927–35.

YÜAN CHEN. *Yüan Chen shih-hsüan.* Ed. Su Chung-hsiang. Shanghai: Ku-tien, 1957.

————. Yüan Chen shih wu-shih-ch'i shou." In *Ts'ai-tiao chi,* ed. Wei Ku. (*SPTK* ed.). Comp. and reproduced in photolithographic ed. Shanghai: Commercial Press, 1920–22.

————. *Yüan-shih Ch'ang-ch'ing chi.* (*SPPY* ed.) Rpt. Kyoto: Chubun shuppan-sha, 1972. (All citations of *YSCCC* are based on this volume.)

————. *Yüan-shih Ch'ang-ch'ing chi pu-yi liu chüan* (*SKCS* Ku-kung shan-pen).

SECONDARY SOURCES

BIRCH, CYRIL, ed. *Studies in Chinese Literary Genres.* Berkeley, Los Angeles, and London: University of California Press, 1974.

CHANG HSIU-YA. "Yüan Chen." In *Chung-kuo wen-hsüeh shih lun-chi,* ed. Chang Ch'i-yün, vol. 2, pp. 399–408. Taipei: Chunghua wen-hua ch'u-pan shih-yeh wei-yüan-hui, 1958.

CHAO KANG. "Yüan Wei-chih *Lien-ch'ang-kung tz'u* fa-wei." *Democratic Review,* 10:17 (September 1959), 20–23; 10:18 (September 1959), 22–24.

CHAO YIN-T'ANG. *Chung-yüan yin-yün yen-chiu.* Shanghai: Commercial Press, 1936.

CH'EN KUEI. "Po Chü-i: People's Poet." *China Reconstructs* (Peking), 2 (July-August 1953), 31–35.

CH'EN LIEN-T'ANG. *T'ang jen shuo hui.* 8 vols. Shanghai: Sao-yeh shan-fang, 1922.

CH'EN YIN-K'O. *T'ang-tai cheng-chih shih shu-lun kao.* Peking, 1956, Rpt. Taipei: Commercial Press, 1966.

————. *Yüan Po shih-chien cheng-kao.* Rev. ed. Rpt. Taipei: Shih-chieh shu-chü, 1955.

————. "Han Yü and the T'ang Novel." *Harvard Journal of Asiatic Studies,* I (1936), 39–43.

————. "The Shun-tsung shih-lu and the *Hsü Hsüan-kuai-lu.*" *Harvard Journal of Asiatic Studies,* 3 (1938), 9–16.

————. *Sui T'ang chih-tu yüan-yüan lüeh-lun kao.* Shanghai: Sheng-huo tu-shu hsin-chih san-lien shu-tien, 1954.

CH'EN YU-CH'IN. *Po Chü-i chuan.* Peking: Chung-hua shu-chü, 1962.

CHENG CHEN-TO. *Chung-kuo wen-hsüeh shih.* Peking: Commercial Press, 1932.

CHIANG SHANG-HSIEN. *Shih-ko hsin-shang.* Taipei: Wen-hsüeh ts'ung-shu, 1960.

CH'IEN MU. *Chung-kuo wen-hsüeh chiang-yen chi.* Kowloon: Jen-sheng ch'u-pan she, 1963.

CH'IEN TUNG-FU. *T'ang Sung ku-wen yün-tung.* Peking: Chung-hua shu-chü, 1965.

CHU TZU-CH'ING. *T'ang shih san-pai shou tu-fa chih-tao.* Taipei: Ch'eng-wen, 1959.

Ch'u-tz'u pu-shu. Ed. Wang I. Taipei: Chung-hua shu-chü, 1966 [*SPPY.*]

Ch'üan T'ang wen. Comp. (ca. 1814) Tung Kao et al. [*SPPY* ed.] Rpt. Taipei: Hua-wen, 1965.

DES ROTOURS, ROBERT. "Les Grands fonctionnaires des provinces en Chine sous la dynastie des T'ang." *T'oung Pao,* XXV (1928), 219–332.

————. *Histoire de Ngan Lou-chan.* Paris: E. Leroux, 1960.

————. *Le Traité des examens.* Paris: Leroux, 1932.

————. *Traité de fonctionnaires et traité de l'armée.* 2 vols. Leiden: E. J. Brill, 1947.

DIÉNY, JEAN-PIERRE. *Aux origines de la poésie classique en Chine.* Lieden: E. J. Brill, 1968.

EBERHARD, WOLFRAM. *Conquerors and Rulers: Social Forces in Medieval China.* 2nd rev. ed. Lieden: E. J. Brill, 1965.

Erh-shih-ssu shih (Po-na ed.). Taipei: Commercial Press, 1968.

FAIRBANK, JOHN K., ed. *Chinese Thought and Institutions*. Chicago: University of Chicago Press, 1957.

FEIFEL, EUGENE. *Po Chü-i as a Censor*. The Hague: Moulton, 1961.

FRANKEL, HANS H. *The Flowering Plum and Hu Palace Lady; Interpretations of Chinese Poetry*. New Haven and London: Yale University Press, 1976.

HANABUSA, HIDEKI. *Gen Shin gōi sakuin kan-ken (Gen Shin ken-kyu I)*. *Kyoto furitsu dai-gaku chūgoku bungaku sōkan* VI. Kyoto: March 1961.

————. *Gen Shin nenpu kō (Gen Shin ken-kyu II)*. *Kyoto furitsu dai-gaku chūgoku būngaku sōkan* VII. Kyoto: October 1962.

————. *Gen Shin sakuhin-shi-ryo-hyo (Gen Shin ken-kyu III)*. *Kyoto furitsu dai-gaku chūgoku bungaku sōkan* IV. Kyoto: July 1958.

————. *Haku Kyo-i kenkyu*. Tokyo: Se-kai shi-so sha, 1971.

————. *Haku-shi Monju no hihanteki kenkyu*. Kyoto: Hoyu shoten, 1974.

HART, HENRY H., tr. *The West Chamber, A Medieval Drama*. Stanford: Stanford University Press, 1936.

HIGHTOWER, JAMES R. "Yüan Chen and 'The Story of Ying-ying.'" *Harvard Journal of Asiatic Studies*, 33 (1973), 90–123.

HOU WAI-LU. *Chung-kuo ssu-hsiang t'ung shih*. Peking: Chung-hua shu-chü, 1964.

HSIAO KUNG-CH'ÜAN. "Ch'en Yin-k'o chih *Yüan Po shih-chien cheng-kao*." *Ch'ing-hua hsüeh-pao*, I (1956), 170–74.

HSIAO YUNG-HSIUNG. *Yüan Po shih-yün k'ao*. Taipei: Wen-shih-che, 1973.

HSIN WEN-FANG. *T'ang ts'ai-tzu chuan*. Shanghai: Lo-t'ien wen-hsüeh ch'u-pan she, 1957.

HSIUNG SHIH-I, tr. *The Romance of the Western Chamber*. London, 1935; rpt., New York: Columbia University Press, 1968.

HSÜ SHIH-YING. "Lun Yüan Chen *Yüeh-fu ku-t'i shih-chiu shou* yung yün." *Tan-chiang hsüeh-pao*, 7 (November 1968), 1–28.

————. "Lun Yüan Chen *Yu-chiu-shih shih-chang* yung yün." *Wen shih chih k'an*, 1 (July 1971), 9–17.

————. "Lun Yüan Chen *Lien-ch'ang-kung tz'u* yung yün." *Wen shih che hsüeh pao*, 15 (August 1966), 397–406.

————. "Lun Yüan Chen *Wang yün chui ko chi Ho Li Chiao-shu hsin-ti yüeh-fu shih-erh shou* yung yün." *Yu shih hsüeh-chih*, 6 (October 1969), 1–23.

HU SHIH. *Pai-hua wen-hsüeh shih*. Shanghai, 1937; rpt. Taipei: Mei-ya, 1969.

—————. "The Social Message in Chinese Poetry." *The Chinese Social and Political Review*, VII (1923), 66–79.

—————. "Yüan Chen Po Chü-i ti wen-hsüeh chu-chang." *Hsin Yüeh*, I (April 10, 1928), 1–27.

HUANG CHENG-MOU. "*Hsi hsiang chi yü Hui chen chi* k'ao-cheng." *Yi-wen chi* 9 (June 1966), 42–44.

HUANG HSÜ-WU. *Shih Tz'u chü chung-t'an*. Taipei: Lo-t'ien ch'u-pan sheh, 1970.

HUNG MAI. *Jung chai sui pi*. Shanghai: Commercial Press, 1934.

KANEKO, HIKOJIRO. *Heian bungaku to hakushi monju*. Tokyo: Baifukan, 1955.

KAO YU-KUNG, and MEI TSU-LIN. "Syntax, diction and imagery in T'ang poetry." *Harvard Journal of Asiatic Studies*, 31 (1971), 49–136.

KATAYAMA, TETSU. *Haku Rakuten*. Tokyo: Iwanami, 1965.

KNECHTGES, DAVID R. *The Han Rhapsody; A Study of the Fu of Yang Hsiung* (53 B.C.–18 A.D.). London and New York: Cambridge University Press, 1976.

KUO MAO-CH'IEN (12th Cent.), ed. *Yüeh-fu shih chi*. 3 vols. Rpt. Taipei: Shih-chieh shu-chü, 1961.

KUO SHAO-YÜ. *Chung-kuo wen-hsüeh p'i-p'ing shih*. Shanghai: Chunghua, shu-chü, 1961.

LAO KAN. *Chung-kuo ti she-hui yü wen-hsüeh*. Taipei, Wen-hsing, 1964.

LEGGE, JAMES, ed. and tr. *The Chinese Classics*. 5 vols. Hong Kong, 1865–1895. Rpt., Hong Kong University Press, 1960.

LEVY, HOWARD S. *Biography of An Lu-shan*. Berkeley: University of California Press, 1960.

—————. *Translations from Po Chü-i's Collected Works*. 2 vols. New York: Paragon Press, 1971.

LIU AN. *Huai-nan-tzu*. (Wu Chin-chuang ed.) Taipei: Chung-hua shu-chü, 1968.

LIU, JAMES. *The Art of Chinese Poetry*. Chicago: Chicago University Press, 1962.

—————. *Chinese Theories of Literature*. Chicago: Chicago University Press, 1975.

LIU SU. *Ta T'ang hsin yü*. (*TSCC* ed.) Rpt. Commercial Press, 1966.

LIU TA-CHIEH. *Chung-kuo wen-hsüeh fa-chan shih*. 3 vols. Hong Kong: Hua-wen, 1961.

LIU WU-CHI. *An Introduction to Chinese Literature*. Bloomington: Indiana University Press, 1966.

—————, and IRVING LO, eds. *Sunflower Splendor*. New York: Doubleday, 1975.

Lo Hsiang-lin. *T'ang-tai wen-hua shih.* Taipei: Commercial Press, 1955.

Lo Ken-tse. *Yüeh-fu wen-hsüeh shih.* Peking: Commercial Press, 1931.

Lu K'an-ju, and Teng Juan-chün. *Chung-kuo shih-shih.* 3 vols. Peking: Tso-chia ch'u-pan she, 1957.

Mizuno, Heiji. *Haku Rakuten to Nikon bungaku.* Tokyo: Meguro shoten, 1930.

Mu t'ien-tzu chuan. Ed. Kuo P'u. (*SPTK* ed.) Taipei: Commercial Press, 1966.

P'ei wen yün fu. Ed. Chang Yü-shu (1042–1711) *et. al.* 6 vols. Rpt. of Palace ed. 7 1711, Peking: Commercial Press, 1908.

Peterson, Charles A. "Corruption Unmasked: Yüan Chen's Investigations in Szechwan." *Asia Major,* 18 (1973), 34–78.

Pulleyblank, Edwin G. *The Background of the Rebellion of An Lu-shan.* London and New York: Oxford University Press, 1955.

––––––. "Neo-Confucianism and Neo-Legalism in T'ang Intellectual Life, 755–806." In *The Confucian Persuasion,* ed. Arthur F. Wright. Stanford: Stanford University Press, 1960.

Rideout, J. K. "The Rise of the Eunuchs During the T'ang Dynasty (618–705)." *Asia Major,* 1 (1949–1950), 53–72; IV (1953) 42–58.

Schafer, Edward H. *The Golden Peaches of Samarkand.* Berkeley: University of California Press, 1963.

––––––. "The Last Years of Ch'ang-an." *Oriens extremes* 10 (1963), 133–79.

––––––. "The Auspices of the T'ang." *Journal of the American Oriental Society,* 83 (1963), 197–225.

Scott, John, ed. and tr. *Love and Protest: Chinese Poems from the Sixth Century B.C to the Seventeenth Century A.D.* New York: Harper and Row, 1972.

Soulié, de Morant. *L'Amoureuse Oriole jeune fille; roman d'amour chinois du xiiime siècle.* Paris: E. Flammarion, 1928.

Ssu-ma Kuang. *Tzu-chih t'ung chien.* Rpt. Taipei: Shih-chieh shu-chü, 1962.

Su Hsüeh-lin. *Chung-kuo wen-hsüeh shih.* Taichung: Kuang-ch'i, 1970.

Ssu-k'u ch'üan shu (Ku-kung shan-pen)—original edition of eighteenth century, n.d. in *MS.* now housed at the Palace Museum of Taipei.

Ssu-pu pei yao. Shanghai: Chung-hua shu-chü, 1927–1935.

Ssu-pu ts'ung-k'an, (ch'u-pien so-pen). Rev. ed. Shanghai: Commercial Press, 1929; rpt. Taipei: Commercial Press, 1965.

Su Shih. *Su Tung-p'o ch'üan chi.* 2 vols. Taipei: Shih-chieh shu-chü, 1964.

Sui-shu. In *Erh-shih-ssu shih,* (*Po-na* ed.) Taipei: Commercial Press, 1968.

T'ai-p'ing kuang-chi. Ed. Li Fang (925–966) et al. Peking, 1959; rpt. Taipei: Hsin-hsing, 1962.

T'ai-p'ing yü-lan. Comp. Li Fang (925–966) et al. 4 vol. Completed in 983. Reproduction of Sung ed. Peking, 1960; rpt. Taipei: Chung-hua shu-chü, 1963.

T'an Cheng-pi. *Chung-kuo wen-hsüeh-chia ta tz'u-tien.* Taipei: Shih-chieh shu-chü, 1962.

Ts'ao P'ei. *Wei Wen-ti chi.* In *Han Wei Liu-ch'ao san-pai chia chi,* ed. Chang P'u (1602–1641). 24 vols. Rpt. Taipei: Hsin-hsing, 1963.

Tu Mu. *Fan-ch'uan wen-chi.* (*SPTK*). Shanghai: Commercial Press, 1920–22.

Tuan Ch'eng-shih (9th century). *Yu-yang tsa-tsu.* Shanghai: Commercial Press, 1929.

Waley, Arthur. *The Life and Times of Po Chü-i.* London: Allen & Unwin, 1949.

———, tr. *Translations from the Chinese.* New York: Knopf, 1945.

Wang Kuang-chi. *Chung-kuo yin-yüeh shih.* Hong Kong: T'ai-ping shu-chü, 1962.

Wang P'u (922–982) comp. *T'ang hui-yao.* (1st ed. 961). 3 vols. Rpt. Taipei: Shih-chieh shu-chü, 1960.

Watson, Burton. *Chinese Lyricism.* New York: Columbia University Press, 1971.

———. *Chinese Rhyme-Prose.* New York: Columbia University Press, 1971.

Wen I-to. *T'ang-shih tsa-lun.* Peking: Ku-chi, 1956.

Wright, Arthur F. and Denis Twitchett, eds. *Perspectives on the T'ang.* New Haven: Yale University Press, 1973.

Yen Nan-fang. "Yüan Chen shih ping-yü." *Wen-hsüeh shih-chieh,* 25 (March 1960), 45–51.

Yen Yü. *Ts'ang-lang shih-hua* (*TSCC* ed.). Shanghai: Commercial Press, 1956.

Yip Wai-lim, ed. and tr. *Chinese Poetry; Major Modes and Genres.* Berkeley and Los Angeles, University of California Press, 1976.

Yü Shou-chen, ed. *T'ang-shih san-pai shou hsiang hsi.* Hong Kong: Chung-hua shu-chü, 1957.

Index

197